ON THE BORDERS OF THE PALE

A History of the Kilgobbin, Stepaside and Sandyford area

RR 0952 **26630X** 1017

Rob Goodbody

Pale Publishing

1993

First published in Ireland in 1993 by
Pale Publishing
Old Bawn
Old Connaught
Bray

ISBN 0 9522663 0 X

Printed in Ireland by Central Remedial Clinic Workshop

Cover design by the Central Remedial Clinic Workshop from a watercolour of Kilgobbin Castle by Gabriel Beranger (1766), courtesy of the National Library of Ireland.

For
Paddy Healy

whose name kept recurring
in the research for this book,
reflecting his huge input
to the archaeology and local
history of this area and of
the Dublin area in general.

CONTENTS

LIST OF PLATES

LIST OF FIGURES

PREFACE

There is no shortage of writings on the history of the area around Sandyford, Stepaside and Kilgobbin. John D'Alton's *History of the County of Dublin*, published in 1838, is still an excellent work, provided one uses it with care. Francis Elrington Ball's *History of the County Dublin* covers Murphystown, Ballyogan and Carrickmines in the first volume, published in 1902; Balally and part of Sandyford in the second volume, published in 1903; and Kilgobbin, Stepaside and Jamestown in the third, published in 1905. Ball's history is generally more reliable than D'Alton, though not infallible. Ball had previously co-written a history of the Parish of Taney, with Everard Hamilton, and this covered the Balally area. He had also written articles on Balally and Murphystown in The *Irish Builder* in 1898. The manuscript history of Kilternan and Kilgobbin produced by the Rector of Kilternan parish, the Rev. O'Murchoe, and published in 1934 after his death, is an excellent work, especially for its wealth of anecdotal detail stemming from the author's intimate familiarity with the area and its occupants. The bibliography at the end of this present work demonstrates the wealth of information available on various topics and by many authors over a considerable period.

However, amongst all the published work there is nothing that attempts a comprehensive overview of the history of all periods in sufficient detail. D'Alton and Ball, good as they are, were attempting histories of the whole county and time and space would have prevented them from producing their work in too much detail. Other writers were able to concentrate on the specific area rather than the whole county, but lacked the scholarship of D'Alton and Ball or else concentrated on specific aspects. In addition to this, there are more recent researches to be drawn upon that were not available when those writers set down their work, particularly in the archaeological aspects.

This book seeks to present a fairly comprehensive history of the area from prehistoric times to the end of the nineteenth century and sometimes a little later. It cannot be totally comprehensive and there still remains work to be done. In particular, the individual histories of the larger houses are barely touched upon and the area considered could be enlarged to encompass much more of the surrounding area if only time and space permitted.

This history is not aimed at the historian. A general failing in works such as D'Alton and Ball is that the authors have to assume that the reader understands the period, events and characters described as it would be impossible to write a local history on that scale while explaining general history under each separate locality. What is attempted in this book, however, is to set the events which make up the district's history into a wider context, giving more of the background. For instance, to someone without a background in history it is of little use to relate the story of the early churches without explaining what was happening to the Church in the wider political context and how other parts of south east Dublin were affected.

While it is hoped that this history will be accessible to the general reader, it is also intended that those who are already familiar with the history of the district will still be able to gain something. There is a substantial amount of original research in this document. In particular, the following aspects have been tackled:

1. Never before has information about so many archaeological finds in this district been compiled into one document.

2. The section of the Pale Ditch at Ballyogan has not appeared in any previous book and was unknown to the archaeological record before the research on this book was carried out.

3. Details of the hierarchy of landowners has not been attempted by previous writers, who tend to mention just one landlord in the chain.

4. While the histories of houses set down in these pages is not as comprehensive as it could be, it is still a more complete list than has been attempted in earlier studies.

In acknowledging that this is not the final word on the history of the area I would welcome any comments on the text from any readers who like it, don't like it, or feel that they have further information.

Rob Goodbody
Old Bawn, Old Connaught, Bray   **25 October 1993**

ACKNOWLEDGEMENTS

A work such as this could not be attempted without the assistance of others and there are several people to whom I am extremely grateful. In the first instance it was Sylvia Dockeray who inspired the study and has put an immense amount of work into it. She and Julian have given me full support throughout the project. Other present and former residents of the area have also helped, particularly Tony and Maureen Walsh, Seamus Rigney, Veronica and David Rowe, John N. Ross and William Richardson.

For my research into the Pale Ditch I am most grateful to Paddy Healy and Dickie Pilkington who gave me their opinions on my opinions. Paddy read through my early drafts of that section and provided helpful comments. He has also provided numerous other snippets of information and has very kindly given me permission to use his superb drawings of the stones at Kilgobbin Church, extracted from his paper published in the *Journal of the Royal Society of Antiquaries of Ireland*. Dickie also checked my earliest draft and was generous with his explanations based on his very detailed examination of the history of the roads in the district.

In one of those delightful coincidences, I had a Pale Ditch at Ballyogan and Kilgobbin, but did not understand why it should be there. Meanwhile, Dr Kenneth Ferguson had a theory that there should be a Pale Ditch in the Sandyford-Kilternan area, but he knew not where. I am grateful to him for introducing me to the writings of Steven G Ellis, which helped to explain the reasons. He also kindly provided early 17th century map evidence for Kilgobbin. I have also received encouragement in relation to the Pale Ditch from Tadgh O'Keefe and Geraldine Stout.

To the staffs of the usual repositories of historical information I should extend the usual thanks. In particular, Tom Gilsenan of the National Archive who took the brunt of the embarrassment when a large amount of copies ordered seemed to be jinxed into never appearing. Similarly, Eugene Hogan of the National Library kept his patience when the fine watercolour by Gabriel Beranger that appears on the cover refused to succumb to his photography until the fourth attempt. Other difficulties which stood in the way of the project ever being completed were the closure of the National

Library for an entire month just as I was getting going and the closure of the National Museum for building works which left many of their records inaccessible. Undaunted, Nessa O'Connor of the Museum's Irish Antiquities Division managed to lay her hands on files on the last day before they were to disappear under polythene for a few months. Christmas also intervened to disrupt the pattern of research, though the staff of the National Library were their usual helpful selves even first thing in the morning after their Christmas party. The staff of the Registry of Deeds also remained courteous and helpful, despite having to open up for two days at the end of December when everyone else was still merrymaking. Geraldine Stout of the Sites and Monuments Record office of the Office of Public Works was also very helpful in providing information in relation to archaeological monuments.

For permission to reproduce material I am grateful to the National Library of Ireland, who provided the prints of Kilgobbin Castle by Gabriel Beranger and George Petrie and have allowed me to use them. I should thank Philip McCann of the Library who persuaded me to get the Beranger done in colour. He was right and it was worth it. I would also like to thank the Reverend David Muir, Rector of Kilternan, for permission to use the extensive quote from the parish's booklet *Kilternan Church 1826 - 1976*.

The production and printing work on the book has been carried out by the Central Remedial Clinic Workshop in Vernon Avenue, Clontarf and I am most grateful to Michael O'Connor, Eamonn McGoldrick and all the staff for adopting the project with a dedication beyond the call of duty!

Finally, it is normal to thank one's wife and family. The task of writing a history of an area from scratch in less than three months while holding down a full time job and meeting all the usual family commitments is a daunting one, and if it was not for Ingrid's tolerance and support, not to mention Aisling, Rory and Ailbhe's understanding, it could not have been done. They continued their support in the ensuing months as the text was amended and improved upon. To the wider family, perhaps you now understand why you saw so little of me over Christmas 1992!

1. INTRODUCTION

The title of this book comes from the passage on Kilgobbin Castle in O Murchoe's *History of Kilternan and Kilgobbin*, published in 1934. The significance of the title will become clear in later chapters when we look at the late medieval castles and sections of the Pale ditch in this district. The book looks at the area around Kilgobbin, Stepaside, Sandyford, Woodside, Barnacullia, Hillcrest Balally and Murphystown, and an area which lies to the south of Dublin city between the suburbs and the mountains. In the east of the area lies The Gallops, which is also being developed for housing at this moment, along with a neighbourhood shopping centre under the title *Leopardstown Valley*. Within a short distance to the north and north east lies the area around Balally and Leopardstown which have seen a great deal of development for housing and industry within the last ten years or so.

To the south and south west lie open farmland and other open land facilities such as a golf course, a pitch and putt course, rugby clubs, and various riding establishments. Further afield lie more of this kind of recreation facility. Along with this lies, incongruously, the rubbish tiphead at Ballyogan, destined in the longer term to be grassed over to extend the golf course. More to the west and further to the south west lie the mountains which provide quarried stone, forestry, recreation and wilderness.

In the middle lie the areas around Kilgobbin, Sandyford, Stepaside, Barnacullia, Woodside and Hillcrest, their future uncertain in many ways. Firstly, there is pressure for development and counter pressure to preserve it against development. Secondly, there is the Southern Cross motorway which, it is proposed, will pass to the north, with another proposal for the South Eastern motorway that may pass through the middle of the area. To return to our title, we find that the area is, once again on the borders of a kind of pale, though this time it relates to the division between suburbia and countryside, and the tensions are not due to the differences between two nations, but to the uncertainties of encroaching development.

In the light of these uncertainties it is worthwhile to think about this district, what it is, and how it has come to be the way that we find it. We can all see that this is an area that has a character that is derived from its history, and this book looks at and explains that history.

In this book the unit of measurement used for the sizes of land holdings is generally the Irish acre or Irish plantation acre. It is convenient to use this measure as it was the one in use at the time. For those who need to know how this compares with today's measurements, a plantation acre was a little over 1.6 statute acres, or roughly equivalent to 0.65 hectares. From time to time the equivalent measurements are given in the text, but for the casual reader it is not important to be precise about the area of a landholding. The rough scale of the plot is all that is needed and the reader should not get tied in knots calculating equivalents.

Something should also be said about administrative areas. Until the end of the nineteenth century the country was divided into districts that differ somewhat from those in use today. The basic unit of administration then, as now, was the *townland*. The townlands in use in the seventeenth and eighteenth centuries were somewhat larger than they are now, and owed their origins to the medieval period or earlier. In the 1830's the Ordnance Survey set down the accurate boundaries of these townlands in greater detail than ever before and also carved some of them up to create new townlands. Woodside, for instance, is an early nineteenth century creation, having previously been part of Kilgobbin townland. Within townlands there may be local placenames that are well known, but whose boundaries have never been fully defined as they have never been official administrative areas. Stepaside and Sandyford are examples, and Woodside was created out of a previously existing area known as The Wood. The principal local placenames mentioned in the text are shown on the map in Figure 1.

Above the townland the next official administrative area was the *parish*. This coincided with the church parish in pre-Reformation days for reasons that will become clearer later. After the Reformation the two churches followed their own ways in terms of parish boundaries, the Catholic church defining totally new areas, while the Church of Ireland held on to the old parish boundaries for a time. These administrative parishes are frequently referred to as *civil parishes* to distinguish them from the ecclesiastical ones that were now no longer the same. At the end of the nineteenth century these parishes were abolished as an administrative unit in favour of Electoral Divisions or District Electoral Divisions. They remain important to the historian, though, as the older official records are classified by parish and, within that, by the townland.

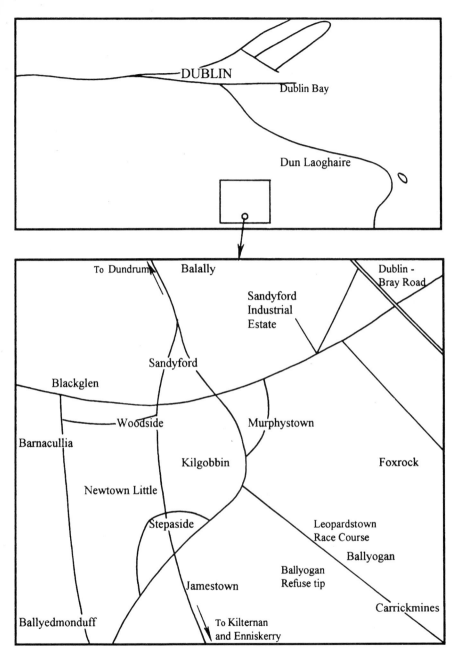

Figure 1: *Location map (not to scale). Showing Principal places mentioned in text*

Above the parish was the *barony*. For local history purposes it is mainly relevant for being the administrative area of the Poor Law Guardians, whose functions included running the local workhouse, and various other functions now operated by the local authorities, such as housing and burial grounds.

This hierarchy can be illustrated by the case of Kilgobbin which is a village, an identifiable area along the Kilgobbin Road that was formerly a town, as we shall hear. It is also a townland, stretching from the new shopping centre on Ballyogan Road as far as Stepaside and the Burrow Golf Course, and including Kilgobbin village and the land around as far as Clay Farm. Kilgobbin was also a parish, made up of the townlands of Kilgobbin, Jamestown, Woodside, Newtown Little (around Fern Hill), Ballyedmonduff, Barnacullia and, in the mountains near Glencullen, Ballybrack townland. Kilgobbin parish lay within the barony of Rathdown which, from the mid 19th century, had its workhouse at Loughlinstown and its burial ground at Deansgrange. Rathdown was divided into two halves, one in Wicklow, extending to Delgany, the other in Dublin. In a number of places in this history the Dublin half barony of Rathdown is taken for comparison of what was happening in the general district around about the area covered in this book, but it is not generally referred to by that name. Instead, the text refers to the area between Rathfarnham and Bray, in order to make it easier for the non-historian to visualise.

Above the barony was, and still is, the *county*. Even these are not static as anyone who has lived in Churchtown for long will testify as part of that area was in County Dublin, was transferred to Dublin City, then back to the county again for a while before the County was carved into three. As far as this area is concerned, the county was Dublin since medieval times, though it now lies within the new county with the contrived name of Dun Laoghaire-Rathdown.

2. PRE-HISTORY AND ARCHAEOLOGY

Comparatively little is known about the early occupiers of Ireland - where they came from, how many they were, how they lived or even how early they came. One thing is certain, though. South east County Dublin is extremely rich in evidence for these early inhabitants. The surviving remains from these periods fall broadly into three categories:- living places, burial places and individual objects. In Ireland, as elsewhere, it is the burial places that are best known, perhaps, including the great passage tombs of Newgrange and Knowth, or the smaller, but still impressive, stone structures such as dolmens. Individual objects or groups of objects are also well known, particularly the spectacular gold ornaments that may be seen in the National Museum of Ireland. Least well known are the living places or occupation sites, as they frequently leave little or no trace above ground and would not usually be recognised by the casual observer if unearthed. However, these are extremely important for our understanding of the lifestyles and the numbers of the early inhabitants of our island. Systematic searches of the ground as has been done along the routes of the various gas pipelines have revealed huge amounts of information from sites that would never have come to light in normal circumstances.

It is not known whether Ireland was visited or occupied by Palaeolithic people. The evidence that they would have left behind would have been minimal and none has been found to date. The more advanced Mesolithic people were certainly here. They were hunters and gatherers living off the natural produce of the land and while the remains they left behind were easily lost and difficult for any but the trained observer to spot, ample evidence has been found for their existence. In the Dublin area Mesolithic sites have been investigated at Sutton and at Dalkey Island and it is possible that other sites may yet be found.

A major revolution occurred with the introduction of farming. This ushered in the Neolithic period which was the time when farming was practised, but without the aid of metal tools. Farming increased the amount of food which could be produced, allowing the population to grow. It also changed the lifestyle of the population by introducing a seasonal cycle in the production of food, with the result that at certain times labour was available for other tasks. One effect of this was the development of structures such as major tombs which were labour intensive in their construction and were something of a luxury in that they were not essential for the survival of life.

There are numerous fine examples of Neolithic structures in the general area considered in this book. Most spectacular are the huge portal tombs, or dolmens, at Kilternan and Brenanstown. In both cases these are constructed of granite with a huge granite capstone weighing up to eighty tonnes. These tombs are not isolated examples. Further down the valley there is another portal tomb at Ballybrack, while others are to be found further west at Larch Hill and Mount Venus and, closer by, at Taylor's Grange.

The Bronze Age is also well represented in the locality. Pride of place must go to the wedge tomb at Ballyedmonduff which dates from around 1700 BC and about which Eugene O'Curry of the Ordnance Survey said in the 1830's that he doubted "if he had ever met so perfect a pagan grave in other counties hitherto examined". It is worth noting that O'Curry was an authority on monuments and, through his work for the Ordnance Survey, had seen plenty of them. There are other Bronze Age wedge tombs at Shankill, Lehaunstown and Kilmashoge, showing that there was a significant Bronze Age presence in the area. There was also a stone circle at Ballybetagh that probably also dated from this period, and a further two stone circles at Ballyedmonduff.

The Iron Age has left us a much more sparse record of monuments, with no great tradition of tomb building and remarkably few identified sites. It is generally thought that *Hill Forts* may date from the Iron Age, but this is uncertain. There are only about eighty of these in Ireland, and one is at Rathmichael, near Shankill. Far more common are *raths*, also known as *raheens* or *ring forts*, and one reason for their abundance is the long period over which they were used. The earliest are of Iron Age origin, while some were occupied throughout the Early Christian period and even into the medieval times. There are plenty of ring forts in the area we are examining in this book. There were three at Jamestown, all now levelled, one at Woodside between Enniskerry Road and Kilgobbin Road, that is still in good condition, and three at Ballyedmonduff. In addition to this there is a very large number of other archaeological enclosures in the vicinity, including no less than ten in Barnacullia and Ballyedmonduff. There is a suggestion that the rath at Woodside is of modern origin, constructed to form a feature in the landscape. While this is known to have been done by some eighteenth century landowners it does not seem likely that Woodside fits into this category as it was never within the landscaped demesne of a big house.

The concentration of monuments around this area is evidence of a strong presence of inhabitants throughout the pre-historic period. Monuments such as these tend to survive better when they are not on arable land and many more may have been destroyed through cultivation. It is uncertain exactly how they and the people that built them were distributed in the area.

Perhaps a better indicator of the distribution of the early inhabitants comes from the finds of archaeological objects. No systematic search for archaeological objects has been undertaken locally, but a surprising number of finds are reported from a range of periods. A few of these date to the Neolithic period, such as the occasional flint arrow-head. A stone axe fell from a lorry load of stone coming from a local quarry in Ballyedmonduff in 1916, while a decorated stone in a style similar to that found in the passage graves was found in Barnacullia in 1968. Excavations at the Brehon's Chair at Taylors Grange revealed a variety of flint implements and some pottery remains dating from the late Neolithic or early Bronze Age period.

Quite a large amount of other material dating from the Bronze Age has appeared locally over the years. In 1927, fragments of an urn were found at Jamestown, along with burned human bones, representing a Bronze Age cremation interment and pieces of another, larger, urn were found nearby along with some teeth and this probably represents another cremation. On another site, at Kilgobbin, an urn was unearthed in the 1830's and probably also dated from the Bronze Age. On yet another site in the heart of Kilgobbin a bronze ring was discovered about twenty years ago. Bronze Age cist graves have also materialised at Jamestown. This is a type of burial where the body is buried in a crouched position in a pit lined with slabs of stone to form a kind of coffin. At Murphystown a bronze flat axe was found in the early 1980's while another was turned up in 1928 at Ticknock mountain. Also in 1928, a copper axe-head was discovered a little further afield, at Newtown, Kilternan.

Items from the Iron Age have been less common in the area, though some remains from this period appeared in the archaeological excavation at the Brehon's Chair at Taylor's Grange.

Archaeological objects from the Early Christian period have been discovered, not surprisingly, at the early church sites in the district. A variety of shaped or decorated stones found at Kilgobbin church will be mentioned later. At Balally, excavations near the site of the old church have produced a strap-tag which possibly dates from the 7th or 8th century, as well as some fragments of later medieval pottery.

Various objects from the medieval period have also surfaced in Kilgobbin and Jamestown, including fragments of three examples of a style of jar known as Bellarmine from three separate locations and a number of other pieces of medieval pottery, also from a spread of sites.

Other archaeological finds have been unearthed in the Kilgobbin-Jamestown area dating from unknown periods, including part of a skeleton of an old man, a small iron tube and numerous fragments of pottery. A stone lined cist was discovered at Jamestown in 1909, though it is not recorded whether human remains or other objects were found in it. In the early 1830's a human skeleton was found in a "massy subterranean dungeon" made of stone in the immediate vicinity of Kilgobbin Castle.

These finds, the principal ones of which from the area of Kilgobbin town are shown on Figure 2, show that the area has been occupied at all periods since at least the Neolithic. The amount of material appearing strongly suggests a significant Bronze Age presence in the immediate area. It also demonstrates the Medieval occupation of the Kilgobbin village area, which will be discussed in more detail in a later section.

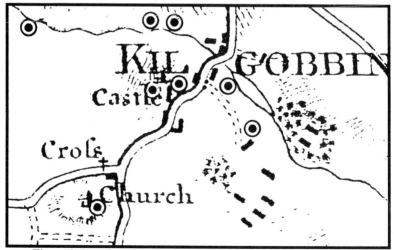

Figure 2: Location of archaeological finds in the Kilgobbin town area.
[map based on Taylor's *Environs of Dublin* (1816)]

3. THE EARLY CHRISTIAN PERIOD

Christianity came to Ireland early in the 5th century AD and spread comparatively quickly. The organisation of the church in Ireland at that time was very different to the parish system which we have today. The early churches were not territorial and were often set up by a lone monk or saint, or, more usually, in the company of a group of his followers. For instance, St Kevin initially lived at Glendalough as a lone ascetic, and only later established a community. Even then, this group was comparatively small and only grew to a large size in later centuries.

There are many Early Christian church sites around the country, and still more have disappeared without trace. In most cases, unfortunately, there is no known history of a church in its early days and the little that is known is gleaned from detective work. This is partly based on the archaeological investigation of whatever remains on the site, partly on any information which may survive in written form, most of which is no earlier than the Norman period, and partly from gleaning information about the saint who may be associated with the church site.

In the area between Rathfarnham and Little Bray more than twenty old church sites are known, virtually all of these seem to have their origins in Early Christian times, though precise information is sparse. In the surrounding district they could be found at Kilternan, Kilmacud, Stillorgan and Dundrum. Within our area there were three, at Balally, Jamestown and Kilgobbin.

The church site at Balally lies within the grounds of the Central Bank premises at Sandyford. Little is known about this church and virtually the only tradition associated with it was that it was built to mark the ending of a feud between two local families. It is thought that this is an eighteenth century tradition, but it gives no clue as to when this event is supposed to have taken place, nor whether it refers to the original foundation of a church on this site or merely to the construction of a new building on an already established site. It is generally accepted that the name Balally refers to a Norse saint, Olaf, which suggests a relatively early date for the church. Reference in a Papal Bull of 1179 to a church called "Ballyvroolef" probably relates to this church. In fact, archaeological excavations carried out at the site of Balally church in 1990 found remains dating from the Early Christian period. Evidence has also been found from air photographs that the church was originally surrounded by a large sub-circular earth bank, and possibly by a double bank. This is the usual arrangement at early church sites and reinforces the idea that Balally church dates from the Early Christian period.

The parish of Kilgobbin is unusual in having two early church sites. Of these, the less well known is Jamestown, where no visible remains of the church survive and where it was forgotten for a time that there had been a church. In fact, even the name of the founding saint was lost in confusion. Each holy well traditionally had a *pattern* once a year, when pilgrims visited to celebrate the feast day of the well's patron saint. The holy well at Jamestown had its pattern on May 1st and in time it was forgotten which saint was celebrated, though the date remained unchanged. May 1st is the feast day of St James and hence is became assumed that James was the patron - hence *Jamestown*. In fact, the patron was St Caoin, brother of St Kevin of Glendalough, as evidenced by the old name for Jamestown, which is *Ballymochain*.

The church site at Jamestown has been lost, but it must have been close to a levelled area which was identified as a burial ground, lying just to the south west of Jamestown cross. The cross, along with the well and burial ground, is in the middle of Stepaside Golf Course, to the front of the ruins of Jamestown House. A sunken laneway, probably of ancient origin, leads away to the north east from the site. The Jamestown cross, well and laneway are in the townland of Kilgobbin.

Kilgobbin Church

Better known than the old church site at Jamestown, and certainly more prominent, is the church of Kilgobbin. Just as with so many of the old church sites, it is difficult to say for how long there was a church at Kilgobbin. The very name of the district suggests an early date for the church, but how old, and who was Gobbin? One tradition is that the founder was the famous master builder, the Goban Saor. This character has been credited with the most remarkable feats of building, not to mention other attributes such as miraculous achievements in metalwork. Legend has placed him in just about every period, crediting him with the great passage tombs such as Knowth and Newgrange, and also with assisting in battles in the Celtic, or Iron Age, period. Perhaps the achievement for which he is best known is the construction of the round towers throughout Ireland, and the legend even goes further to credit him with the building of medieval castles and abbeys, including Kilgobbin Castle. George Petrie, the 19th century antiquarian, believed that the Goban Saor lived in the 7th century and came from near Swords in north County Dublin. There is no particular reason why a 7th century Goban Saor should not have established a church at Kilgobbin, and perhaps the location is a good one, adjacent to the source of good granite. However, there is no supporting evidence for this tradition.

Another possible candidate who has been suggested is the Kerry saint who established Kilgobbain, near Tralee. This man was a nephew of St David of Wales and in the light of this it may seem to be no coincidence that in the earliest mention of the church of Kilgobbin, in 1179 AD, it was referred to as *Techbretnach*, a name which was later translated by Archbishop Alen as "the house of the Welshmen (called Kilgobbin)". However, one should not stretch coincidence too far, as Welsh monks or saints were not uncommon in Early Christian times.

In his *History of the County Dublin* Francis Elrington Ball states that the church "is said to owe its foundation to St Gobban, whose festival falls on April 1st". In fact, there are no less than five saints in the Irish calendar with names similar to Gobban and the truth about the dedication of this church may never be known, while its date may also remain a mystery.

There is no doubt, however, that this is a pre-Norman church site. The documentary evidence is the mention of the church as in existence in 1179, immediately following the arrival of the Normans, while in recent years physical evidence has come to light to support the pre-Norman origin. The church is in the care of the local authority and in 1983 a programme of maintenance and repair work was carried out on the church and churchyard by Dublin County Council. The porch on the north side of the church was considered to be in poor structural condition and was taken down and rebuilt. The porch had originally had two doors, but that on the eastern side had been blocked up. The lintol of this blocked up door attracted attention as it was too slim to have been designed for the purpose. When it was removed it was found to be a grave slab with geometric patterns rather than an inscription. This is a slab of a type found at various early church sites in the area, including Rathfarnham, Whitechurch, Tully and Rathmichael and they are generally thought to date from the Viking period, though this does not imply that they were carved by Vikings or for them. There may not have been Vikings actually living in the Kilgobbin area. A fragment of another slab of this type was also found, this one lying in the graveyard. A piece of a small Early Christian cross was also discovered, consisting of one of the arms from the head of the cross. These stones are shown in Figure 3.

Amongst the other stones which were discovered at this time were some notched pieces of granite of unknown purpose, but which may have been part of the structure of an earlier church on the site. These stones are now displayed in the rebuilt porch of the church, while the stone slabs are fixed to the wall inside the church.

These were not the first finds at Kilgobbin church. The cross which stands in the laneway near the church is said to have been discovered in the early 19th century when a grave was being dug. It is marked as standing in its present position on Taylor's map of the Environs of Dublin, published in 1816 (see Figure 10).

Kilgobbin Cross

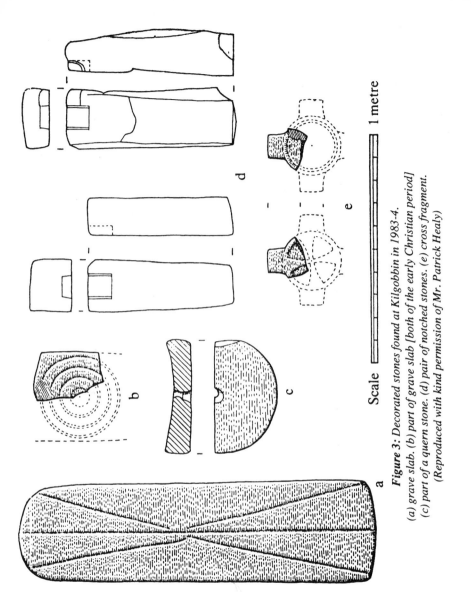

Figure 3: *Decorated stones found at Kilgobbin in 1983-4.*
(a) grave slab. (b) part of grave slab [both of the early Christian period]
(c) part of a quern stone. (d) pair of notched stones. (e) cross fragment.
(Reproduced with kind permission of Mr. Patrick Healy)

Scale ▬▬▬ 1 metre

This cross stands about 2.5 metres high and is carved on both faces. One arm is missing, and may yet be discovered still buried in the grave yard. The base of the cross is a flat slab of granite and has a hollowed-out basin which is a feature common in Early Christian times, particularly at church sites, known as a *bullaun*. It is not certain whether this cross base was placed in its present position when the cross was found, or whether, as often happens, it had remained on its original site, devoid of cross, for a considerable period. The cross is believed to date from about the ninth or tenth century.

The site of Kilgobbin church is spectacular, standing proudly on the top of a steep hillock. The strikingly steep sides of the mound have led some to believe that it is artificial, and possibly either a Norman *motte* or a Neolithic passage tomb. However, while the hillock was artificially shaped, the truth about its origins is less spectacular. The church was built on a low natural ridge of gravel resulting from the processes of the ice age. In the 18th and 19th century this gravel was exploited by quarrying, thereby removing just about all of the part of the hillock that was not occupied by the churchyard. The result has been a massive decrease in the area of the hill and a consequent increase in its steepness.

This quarrying avoided the then existing church site, but ignored the original extent of the ecclesiastical enclosure. As this church dated from the Early Christian period it would originally have been sited within a sub-circular enclosure considerably larger that the present walled churchyard. If any of this remained after the quarrying it was probably to the north of the church, where the newer graveyard now stands. There is a noticeable low ridge running through the graveyard that is best seen in the way that the back wall rises up to cross it. This ridge may be part of the original surrounding enclosure. Recent cutting into the hillside to create level sites for new graves has disturbed bones in the soil, demonstrating that the wall around the old churchyard is of comparatively modern construction and bears no relation to the original boundaries of the churchyard. There is a report that the wall was constructed at the time that the cross was unearthed, which would date it to the early years of the 19th century.

As we will see later, the church building is not of early date. The original church would probably have been of timber if built in the 7th century. It would have been replaced at some stage by a stone structure which lasted until the seventeenth century.

4. THE MEDIEVAL PERIOD AND THE CASTLES

The early Norman period

In many areas of south County Dublin, as elsewhere, the early part of the period after the arrival of the Normans is frequently somewhat hazy. Various names of the landowners are known at intervals but no complete picture emerges as to precisely when and how any of these people acquired their property. In some cases it may have been by inheritance, but in the absence of genealogical information little can be said about this. There are considerable gaps in time during which it is not known who was in either ownership or occupation.

The discovery of carved grave slabs dating from the Viking era, around the tenth to twelfth centuries, at the old church of Kilgobbin shows that there was a significant presence of occupiers here at that time. However, it is not clear what happened to the land ownership following the Norman invasion is not clear, though. In many parts of the general area there is definite information about the colonisation of the district by Norman lords. At Dundrum, for instance, a fairly complete list of Norman occupiers is known from the time of the invasion in the twelfth century through to the arrival of the Fitzwilliams in the fourteenth century, and whose descendants became the modern ground landlords. In other places, however, including the whole area around Kilgobbin, the story is less complete.

In the thirteenth century Sir John Harold was known to have possessed the land of Kilgobbin. The Harold family was of Norse origin and it is generally believed that much of the area around the foothills of the Dublin mountains was held by the descendants of Viking families. The Harold family, in particular, is commemorated in names such as Harold's Cross and, nearer to our area, Harold's Grange. The Harolds do not seem to have been here since Viking times, however, and appear to have taken their lease at the beginning of the thirteenth century from the Hacket family. The Hackets may have been connected with the Harolds, as Sir William Hacket had acted as guardian to Peter Harold. The Hackets may also have occupied Kilgobbin before leasing it to the Harolds.

Another family connected with Kilgobbin in the earlier period after the Norman invasion were the Howells, but the precise timing of their arrival and departure is not known.

The Castles

While the land ownership over time may be vague, information as to how many people lived in this area, and in what sort of buildings, is even more so. We can hazard a guess that the settlement of Kilgobbin was somewhere in the vicinity of the church, quite possibly in or around the site of the later castle. In some parts of the surrounding district it is known that there was a castle soon after the arrival of the Normans. For instance, the castle at Shankill dates from the thirteenth century. It was known that the castle at Dundrum is of comparatively late date and that there had been an earlier one on the site, also dating from the thirteenth century. The remnants of this earlier castle reappeared in recent years as a result of an archaeological excavation and have proved to be far more extensive than had been anticipated. Closer to our area there was an early castle at Carrickmines.

Carrickmines Castle

Carrickmines Castle is one of the more neglected of the historical sites in south Dublin as little now remains. The surviving fragment of the gate house has been mentioned in a number of books, but these tend not to delve further into the history of the castle and even its actual site is not certain. The Ordnance Survey marks a site on its maps, but the surveyors visited the site almost two hundred years after the castle was destroyed and there had been farm buildings here for a considerable period prior to the survey. It is unlikely, then, that any precision lay behind the placing of the symbol for the site of the castle on the maps.

In fact, Carrickmines Castle was an early Norman castle. There are accounts of various forces that were stationed at Carrickmines Castle in its earlier days, including a troop of light horsemen in 1360, a large force in 1375, forty mounted archers in 1388 and a troop of horse in 1593. This quite clearly paints a picture of a castle of considerably greater size and importance than the later tower houses such as Kilgobbin and Murphystown. The area around the castle was examined some years ago by an archaeologist, Patrick Healy and he found quite significant traces of outworks that had been part of the castle defences. These included the remains of three fosses, or ditches, and two earth banks 67 metres long forming what he said "must have been a formidable defensive feature".

As will be seen in a later chapter, Carrickmines Castle saw action in the 1641 rebellion and was later destroyed, leaving only the fragment of a gate house standing. It is said that the castle was blown up and levelled with the ground following the battle and this seems to accord with the Civil Survey. This was compiled in 1654, twelve years after the battle and after the end of the rebellion, and states that there was the wall of a castle in existence at Carrickmines. This could well refer to the fragment of the gate house that may still be seen today. However, a large structure is depicted on the Down Survey of 1655 and if this is not Carrickmines Castle it would seem to relate to some other very substantial building.

Tower Houses

Unlike Carrickmines, Shankill and the first Dundrum Castle, most of the castles in the area between Rathfarnham and Bray date from the later medieval period and are, more correctly, *tower houses* rather than castles. While many of these areas were occupied in the earlier medieval period before these tower houses were built, early medieval remains have generally not yet been discovered.

Kilgobbin Castle

Tower houses are generally all of a type, being comparatively small castles. The Norman occupation of Ireland had spread quite rapidly through the country during the late 12th century but had failed to make a permanent conquest. Over the ensuing years much of the territory gained initially was gradually lost. The reasons for this are many, but perhaps the principal ones were, firstly, that Ireland had never been a single political entity and so a conquering force had to overcome each individual tribal unit individually, with a consequently huge commitment of time, forces and expenditure. Secondly, Ireland was not allocated sufficient reserves or attention by most of the medieval kings, particularly during the Hundred Years' War with France and during the Wars of the Roses, when military resources were occupied elsewhere.

As a result, by the later 14th century the English presence in Ireland was dispersed and diluted such that the only remaining area wherein the king's writ remained strong was in the east, in County Dublin and parts of the surrounding counties of Louth, Meath and Kildare. The edges of this stronghold were under constant threat of attack by the neighbouring Irish clans and despite various protective measures incursions took place from time to time, usually with great damage to property. From the late 14th century, and more particularly during the 15th century, a number of tower houses were built as part of the defence of the area. Ultimately, there were about thirty of these built in the area between Rathfarnham and Bray, in addition to the seven in the town of Dalkey. Each of these was more of a fortified house than a garrisoned castle, though some were larger than others. It was normal for these tower houses to have a walled enclosure attached, known as a *bawn*, and this was for the safety of animals such as cattle during a raid.

The construction of tower houses accelerated from the year 1429, when an act of parliament provided for a subsidy of £10 towards their construction. The reason for the subsidy was that the defence they offered was not just to the benefit of the occupant but also helped to maintain the amount of land in the control of the Anglo-Norman settlers in general. If a landowner could remain in possession of his land against attack from the native Irish it would be to the ultimate benefit of the colony. The castles did not form a line, as is often implied, as there was no concept at this time of controlling access by way of a border or barrier. Instead, the castles were dotted everywhere, on each major landholding, right up to the edge of the city.

Kilgobbin Castle

At Kilgobbin, the Walsh family was in occupation by this time, and it is generally presumed that this family built the castle. Various branches of the Walsh family came into possession of a large amount of land in south east County Dublin during the medieval period, and they were responsible for the building of quite a number of castles, while they occupied others built by their predecessors in title. Thus it was that they held an almost continuous line of castles between here and Bray, including Balally, Kilgobbin, Carrickmines, Brenanstown, Shanganagh, Corke and Old Connaught.

Kilgobbin Castle, 1766, by Gabriel Beranger

The original appearance of Kilgobbin castle itself is quite well established. There is a fine watercolour of the castle taken by Gabriel Beranger in 1766 when the ruins were comparatively complete. While Beranger tended to be faithful to detail in the buildings he depicted, he was not the finest of draughtsmen. However, if his watercolour is examined in conjunction with the engraving by George Petrie executed in about 1819, a comparatively complete picture of the east, north and south sides of the castle may be seen. Comparison with the remains visible today reveals a substantial amount of information on the original layout and construction of the castle.

Kilgobbin Castle, 1819, by George Petrie

Kilgobbin Castle was, in many ways, typical of the tower houses in the south Dublin area. On the ground floor was a single room, the ceiling of which was vaulted. A significant amount of this vaulting can be seen today. While most of the castles of the period were vaulted very few examples of vaulting survive in this district. Dundrum and Puck's Castles were not vaulted, while castles such as Shanganagh and Murphystown only partly survive and the vaulting has gone. Also typical of the tower houses around Dublin is the corner tower which projects from the southern face of the castle at its eastern corner. This projection held the staircase. At the top of the tower part of the crenellation or battlements may be seen and this is in the typical stepped form which was common in Ireland. Some of the windows of the castle survive and others may be seen in the views carried out by Beranger and Petrie. Some of these were simple *loops* suitable for firing on an enemy, while others were somewhat larger. The *Civil Survey* of 1654 stated that the castle was thatched, as were many others in the vicinity. It is not known whether it was thatched or slated originally, but it would seem likely that the thatch was original.

Vaulting at Kilgobbin Castle

Although it was unoccupied by the eighteenth century, Kilgobbin Castle remained substantially intact for many years. As can be seen in the illustrations by Beranger and Petrie a large vertical fissure developed on the eastern side, near to the south eastern corner. However, this fissure has since been repaired. Other cracks seem to be apparent in Petrie's view, and one of these may have developed into a more serious structural failure, as a large part of the castle fell in 1834. When the historian John D'Alton visited the castle in 1837 he found that the principal part of the structure lay in mortared masses over its former court. A description of the remains of the castle in 1835 states that it was "unclothed with ivy, unveiled by trees", quite the opposite to its state in sixty years later when E R McC Dix examined the castle but regretted how little of it was visible due to it being hidden behind trees and clothed with a dense cover of ivy.

It is uncertain whether the castle had a bawn. The *Civil Survey* mentioned a garden plot associated with the castle and this garden continued to be mentioned in papers relating to Kilgobbin in the eighteenth century. The doorway from the castle led through the western face of the building, suggesting that the garden was on that side. As many of the castles of the area had a bawn attached it is more than likely that there was one here. The intensive farming of the area would be likely to ensure that a disused bawn would be swept away to create additional land and if this was the case it is probable that this was also on the western side.

There are several stories relating to treasure being hidden at Kilgobbin Castle. Two of the upstairs rooms were known locally as *money rooms* and were supposed to have treasure hidden in them. One tradition had it that the Goban Saor, the legendary builder of the castle, had concealed his wealth in the building before leaving to work in France, never to return. Various stories were told of local people who had come upon wealth inexplicably, including one farmer named Moran who discovered the supernatural secrets of the hidden treasure in a dream and having laid his hands on it moved away from the district to keep his secret. This could not refer to George Moran, one time innkeeper at Kilgobbin, as he died while still living locally. Nor could it have referred to his brother who farmed at Jamestown, as he ran into financial difficulties. It is also unlikely to refer to their father, Edmund Moran as the family remained in the district. A Thomas Moran later had a part share in the inn and may have been George Moran's son. He is a possible candidate as he moved out of the district to live in west Wicklow. Another possibility is Marks Moran who held land in the field to the rear of the castle in the late eighteenth century. The castle was out of use by the middle of the century, as seen in Beranger's watercolour, and Austin Cooper, a well known antiquary, wrote in 1780 that the castle was in a very poor state, adding that the local people said that people from Dublin had recently been digging there at night and had discovered treasure.

There are also ghost stories associated with Kilgobbin Castle. At night a man in heavy armour is reported to pass by the doors of the cottages which formerly stood close to the castle. A woman in white is also reported to go to the ruins of the castle and emerge with something, apparently gold, in her apron. In addition to these, the story of Mr Moran and his treasure claims that the treasure was guarded by an elf.

While it would seem to be expected that an ancient structure such as this would have stories of treasure and ghosts attached to it, it is worth noting that other castles in the district do not tend to be the subject of this kind of legend. Whether this adds credence to the stories is a matter of opinion.

Balally Castle

William Walsh of Carrickmines was granted land at Balally by the Crown in 1407, subject to a condition that he build a small castle there. This was not an uncommon condition and a similar one was applied to lands at Shanganagh which were leased in the following year by the church. In fact, the castle was not built immediately, but nevertheless the Walsh family not only built it, but occupied it for more than two hundred years.

All traces of this castle have disappeared long since and even its site is never mentioned in any of the histories. It seems, however, to have been on the left hand side of the road leading from Dundrum to Sandyford, where the Balally estate is now. Like many tower houses of the period, Balally castle was thatched. The Hearth Tax roll for 1664 shows that it had three hearths, which suggests that it was a good sized tower house.

Murphystown Castle

Very little is known about Murphystown Castle. The townland was known in the past as Mulchanstown and the castle appears under this name on the Down Survey map of this area which was produced in the 1650's but it was not mentioned in the Civil Survey of 1654. Although it is not known who built this castle or when, it would seem to be a tower house of the type built around the fifteenth century. It has been in ruins for many years. In 1775 it was sketched by Gabriel Beranger who showed that all that survived at that time was part of the ground floor with a large amount of one wall missing. Through the resulting gap could be seen the barrel vaulting that is so typical of tower houses of the time.

The historian, Francis Elrington Ball, stated in 1898 that Beranger's sketch showed Murphystown Castle "to have been then in much the same state of ruin as it is at present". He had obviously not examined the ruin, and corrected this statement in his *History of the County Dublin*, published in 1902, where he says "as the picture shows, ruins of much greater size were visible". In fact, by the end of the nineteenth century only a part of one wall survived, with a short length of an adjoining wall. The ruin was described in detail in an article by E R McC Dix in the *Irish Builder* in 1897 and from his description it seems that little has changed to the present day. In fact, the remains he described resemble the castle as it was shown on the first edition of the Ordnance Survey 6 inch map in 1843, and it seems, therefore, that the fragment of the castle that survives has been in its present state for at least 150 years. It now stands within the grounds of Glencairn, close to the driveway, and can be seen from Murphystown Road.

5. THE PALE DITCHES

Although a substantial number of tower houses had been built around Dublin and the surrounding counties by the late fifteenth century, their effectiveness generally was limited to the protection of the people occupying them and whatever goods and animals were held in the castles or in a bawn attached.

South County Dublin suffered from periodic attacks by the O'Byrne and O'Toole families that were based in the depths of the Wicklow hills at Glenmalure and Glendalough. From time to time the various tracts of land in the area were described as "of no value" or "laid to waste" as a result. Thus the English enclave may have been predominantly English but it certainly was not entirely secure.

This English enclave became known as the Pale or the English Pale, probably by analogy with the similar situation that existed at the English Pale around Calais. The word *Pale* is from the Latin word for a stake and seems to derive from the method of protective fencing using vertical stakes. Similar words used today are *palisade* and *paling*.

The land within the Pale which was entirely under the control of the English settlers was known as the *maghery* and surrounding this was a kind of buffer zone called the *march*. In 1488 the boundaries of the maghery were defined as stretching from Dalkey to Merrion and then to the Dodder, and on to Saggart, Rathcoole, Kilteel, Rathmore, Ballymore Eustace, Naas, Clane, Kilcock and Dundalk. It will be seen from this that most of south County Dublin was excluded from that area, apart from a coastal strip. Part of this line at Merrion still existed into the twentieth century. This line is often quoted as being the line of The Pale, however, at other times different boundaries are given, for instance, in 1515, as running from Dalkey to Tallaght and thereby including some of south Dublin such as Monkstown and Clonkeen, a substantial amount of which would have been excluded by the earlier line.

In 1494, an Act of Parliament was passed requiring landowners to construct a new line of defence along the borders of the Pale. They were to be assisted by every inhabitant, earth tiller and occupier. This defence was to take the form of a "double ditch of six feet high above ground on one side ... which mireth next unto Irishmen". What this meant was the construction of a pair of ditches with a high bank between them. The object of the exercise was to give some form of protection to the entire area rather than just at the tower houses. It was not intended that this should be an impassable Berlin Wall, but merely a hindrance to movement. One of the principal sources of wealth at the time was cattle and the Pale ditch was intended to obstruct the theft of cattle from within the Pale for long enough to allow for resistance to be mustered.

Despite the legal requirements it is doubtful whether this defence work was ever completed and so little of it remains that it is difficult to understand how it could have offered any defence at all. The sheer scale of the ditch makes it seem unlikely that it could disappear without trace or that is could be overlooked. The ditches are often three metres wide and up to two metres deep, while the bank is so large that its broad, flat top can be used as a trackway and there is even a section of it in Co Kildare that has a tarmacadamed road running along the top of the bank. They are also linear in nature, and would be of little use if they did not extend over a significant distance. However, three issues arise here. Firstly, it appears that the responsibility for the construction of the Pale ditch rested with the individual landowners. It is quite possible then, that the ditch could have been constructed in some places and not in others that were equally at risk. Secondly, there is every possibility that sections of the ditch could have been destroyed deliberately in later years, perhaps even a high percentage of the original length. W G Tempest, writing in 1941, quoted a farmer of his acquaintance as saying that he himself levelled part of the ditch "to facilitate the planting of trees, tillage and saving obvious waste from so large a bank". It should be noted that this farmer referred to himself as an antiquarian, though this did not stand in the way of his agricultural improvement. How readily, then, ditches could have been destroyed by non-antiquarians. Thirdly, despite the sheer scale of the ditch, sections of it have remained unrecognised until recently in areas that were well known to archaeologists and local historians. It is very possible that there are other sections, still in existence, that have yet to be recognised as the Pale ditch. This failure to identify the ditch is understandable when one considers that the precise line of the defence is not known and it may be some considerable distance from its expected location. The line of the Pale also varied over time, and it is probable that two sections of it may exist in one area that were never connected together and that represent separate alignments from different periods.

The relevance of the Pale to the our area is not immediately apparent when one examines maps which show the supposed alignment of the Pale ditch. These invariably depict the feature as running from the Merrion area to Dalkey not far in from the coast, as set down in 1488. This is a curious route to take, as it excludes large quantities of good land while leaving a narrow coastal band to with a long boundary to be defended. However, as we have noted, this was the boundary of the *maghery*. Beyond this lay the *march* which was protected by its own Pale ditch. Francis Elrington Ball and Everard Hamilton in their book *The Parish of Taney* published in 1895, considered the question of the Pale at length, based on a note by the Rev. G T Stokes. Unfortunately, no source is given for Stokes's opinions, but the route is described in detail: "The Pale began at Dalkey and followed a south-westerly direction towards Kilternan; then turning northwards passed Kilgobbin, where a castle still stands, and crossed the Parish of Taney to the south of that part of the lands of Balally now called Moreen, and thence in a westerly direction to Tallaght, and so on to Naas in the Co of Kildare". The description goes on to describe a watch-tower and the remains of a guard-house adjoining it in the boundary wall of Moreen, now the site of the Central Bank premises at Sandyford, implying that these buildings were part of the Pale defences. The tower was not of medieval date, however, and it is probable that the "guard house" was also a later structure. It is said that the "guard house" was used as a tea house by the residents of Moreen and it seems likely that the tower was built as a viewing tower and that they were erected in the 18th century.

Pale Ditch at Kilcross, Balally

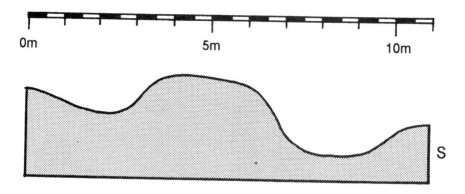

Section 1:   47 metres east of farm laneway

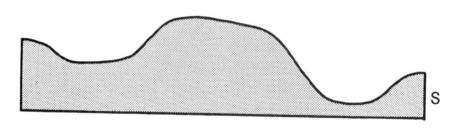

Section 2:   c.100 metres east of farm laneway

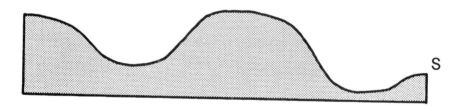

Section 3:   24 metres from east end of ditch

Figure 4: *Cross sections through earthwork*

It is curious that Ball and Hamilton did not identify any portions of the actual Pale ditch, particularly as there is a local tradition that the Pale passed through the area. There is a section of it at the Kilcross estate, on land that was originally in the grounds of Moreen, the house that also had the supposed watch tower and guard house in its demesne. During the construction of the Kilcross estate in the mid 1970's local people alerted the builder to the significance of the feature and an archaeologist, Patrick Healy, was called in. He found that the ditch was about 220 metres long with a flat topped bank flanked by two ditches. The bank was up to 4 metres wide at the top, 6 metres wide at the base and with ditches averaging about 2 metres wide.

The present writer has identified another, longer and better preserved section of the Pale ditch at Ballyogan. This is in the form of a high flat-topped bank with large ditches on both sides. The bank is generally between two and three metres wide on top and stands up to two and a half metres above the present bottom of the ditches. The ditches vary from two metres to three metres wide . It appears that the depth of the ditches was originally greater, but erosion of the bank has gradually partly filled them. The ditch on the northern side is generally shallower as it is on the uphill side and would have suffered from the gradual washing of soil down the significant slope of the adjoining field. There are hedgerow trees growing on the bank and some of them, particularly hawthorn, appear to be of great age. Some cross-sections of it are shown in Figure 4.

Pale Ditch at Ballyogan

This ditch or earthwork stretches for a length of 500 metres, with three breaks through it, one being a farm lane, one is an access between fields, and the third is where a sewer has been laid in recent years. It is almost perfectly straight, except that at its eastern end it curves slightly towards the nearby river. At the western end it meets the edge of Ballyogan tiphead and it seems that it may have extended further westwards. The position of this ditch is good for defensive purposes. It lies at the edge of the flat floor of the valley which, even now, is damp, and must have been fairly marshy in medieval times. This marshy area and the river beyond it lie to the south of the ditch, which is the side facing towards the Irish tribes which the ditch was intended to keep out.

The alignment of the feature is also good for defence. It lies on a line between Carrickmines and Kilgobbin, both of which had castles which were owned by the Walsh family at the time that Pale ditches were constructed. At the Carrickmines end the ditch finishes near the river just short of the extensive earthworks at Carrickmines Castle. In the opposite direction it seems to have originally continued to Kilgobbin as stated by Ball and Hamilton. John Rocque's map of County Dublin dated 1760 (Figure 9) shows a footpath or trackway leading along here from Carrickmines directly to the farmhouse where Greenfield House now stands, near to Kilgobbin. The broad, flat top of pale ditches made excellent pathways and it is likely that this ditch served that purpose before the building of Ballyogan Road in the nineteenth century.

Along the southern boundary of the grounds of Greenfield House there is another bank and ditch that would warrant close examination. It does not conform to the usual style of Pale Ditch but this may be because of the lie of the land. The ground falls away from the south towards the river which runs from Kilgobbin to Carrickmines and there is a sharp drop in level of up to 5 metres. About half way down this slope there is an earth bank which has been formed by excavating out a ditch on the uphill side. Where the slope is less significant there are ditches on both sides. It is hard to see what function this substantial feature would form given that the ditches could not form any drainage function on this slope and livestock can be better controlled by lesser features. The bank itself is not as large as the typical Pale Ditch banks, but nevertheless it would seem quite possible that this is the origin of the bank and ditches. Its alignment would fit in very well with the direction of the Ballyogan Pale Ditch. The section of the Ditch at

Ballyogan and Kilgobbin are shown in in Figure 5.

It appears that the Pale ditch turned from the boundary of Greenfield House to head towards Kilgobbin Castle. There is a reference in a deed dating from 1727 to a plot of land in Kilgobbin "where the old ditch was to be thrown down and a sufficient road left to William Webb's house". William Webb lived in a house near where Kilgobbin Cottage stands today and it appears that this deed refers to the lane which still leads off Kilgobbin Road to Kilgobbin Cottage and Clay Farm. This reference may refer to the destruction of part of the Pale ditch where it ran between Greenfield House and Kilgobbin Castle. It seems to be no coincidence that if these two buildings are joined with a line on a map this line would coincide with the northern end of this lane where it is at a different angle to the rest of the lane. This change of direction is not due to the presence of the farm house which adjoins it as it is of considerably later date than the lane. It is probably also no coincidence that the adjoining river briefly changes direction to run along the same alignment, and perhaps this, too, is a relic of the old Pale ditch. Thus the section of the ditch on the southern boundary of Greenfield runs alongside the river and turns sharply westward, with the river also turning here, and passes along the northern edge of the laneway on its way to the castle.

There is no contradiction involved in having a well defined line of the Pale passing close to the coast and another line through Ballyogan, Kilgobbin and Balally. In fact, these two lines seem to represent the borders of the *maghery* and the *march* respectively. It is more than likely that the line of the Pale varied significantly over time, but in this case it is quite possible that the two lines were both present at the same time, representing two separate features.

There are still questions over how one section of this Pale Ditch would connect with the next. What happens to it after Kilcross? How did Kilcross connect with Kilgobbin? It is possible that this link led over the edge of the mountain. At the top of Slate Cabin Lane there is a short section of a large bank at a point which is known locally as "The Town Gate", and tradition has it that this was an exit from the Pale onto the mountains. At Barnacullia there is a local belief that part of a footpath known as Glovers Lane follows a part of the ditch. While it seems difficult to fit these in to a logical alignment for the Pale Ditch there is a need for a more detailed examination of this area to look at what remains on the ground and, more importantly, to gather the strands of local tradition. After all, it was local tradition that kept alive the possibility of a Pale Ditch in this area long after it was forgotten to history, and this led to the finding of the portion of the ditch at Kilcross. This shows that the information handed down through the generations should not be ignored or dismissed lightly in the quest for the other portions of the ditch.

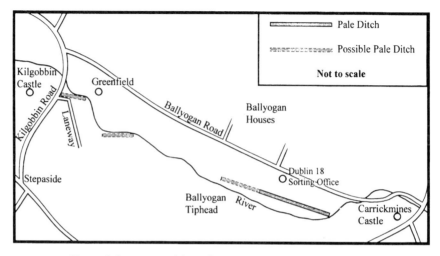

Figure 5: Locations of the Pale Ditch at Kilgobbin and Ballyogan

6. THE SEVENTEENTH CENTURY AND REBELLION

The late sixteenth and early seventeenth centuries was not a good time for Catholicism. After the initial period following the Reformation, when there was a certain amount of confusion over the differentiation between the two denominations, the reign of Queen Elizabeth I brought moves against Catholics. Hopes that the accession of James I to the throne would lead to an easing off of persecution proved to be ill-founded.

The "old English" families in Ireland, such as the Walshes of Kilgobbin and the surrounding district, found themselves in an anomalous position. They had been part of the English-based settlement of Ireland and had looked to England for support and cultural identity. Increasingly over the years they had drifted away from their roots, to the extent that they had not taken on the new Anglican religion along with their counterparts in England, but had held on to their Catholicism.

The seventeenth century also brought Puritanism which grew in strength and power in England. As the puritan element in parliament began to run into conflict with the king this led the "old English" in Ireland into another problem. Their natural instinct was to take the side of the king as there was a strong likelihood that a puritan parliament would adopt more draconian measures against Catholicism. However, the concept of Catholic loyalism was not received enthusiastically. Instead, the "old English" found themselves in alliance with the native Irish, the bond of a common religion proving stronger in the circumstances than their disparate origins.

The Rebellion

The first violence erupted in Ulster in October 1641 when the Catholic population rose up against the Protestant settlers. It must be remembered that the Ulster plantation had taken place only thirty years before and the resentment must have been strong amongst the local native population. However, this rebellion was not confined to Ulster. It had been planned as a widespread uprising but, as so often with rebellions in Ireland, the plot was uncovered at the last moment and the leaders arrested. The Ulster wing of the rising having started, the affair spread quickly southwards. This was a particularly bloody rebellion with atrocities being committed by both sides. Rumours spread quickly that large numbers of Ulster Protestants had been massacred and this, in turn, led to a strengthening of the support for the puritan cause in England, helping to move towards the Civil War.

The area around Dublin was not immune to rebellion. The former concept of The Pale had lost its significance in the light of the new alliance between the old English and the native Irish, as the former lords of the pale very quickly decided to side with the rebels. While there were no large scale massacres or atrocities as rumoured elsewhere, there certainly were outrages committed. The vicar's house at Rathmichael was attacked and when the vicar took refuge in Lehaunstown castle the castle was attacked and set on fire. At Kill of the Grange the Church of Ireland curate's house was attacked and his wife and a servant abducted and hanged. While no such atrocities are recorded from our area, unrest was present. A widow living at Murphystown lodged a complaint that her property had been stolen by the occupant of Kilgobbin Castle, Matthew Talbot. This is not a major incident in the context of the rebellion as a whole, but it illustrates the troubles of the time. By the end of 1641, the whole of south County Dublin was in rebel hands.

The first moves to retaliate against the rebels to the south of Dublin took place in the middle of January 1642. Dundrum Castle was one of those that had been taken by the rebels and in that month a party of troops marched from Dublin and retook this castle. On the same day, a force of cavalry moved on Kilgobbin Castle. Matthew Talbot, the tenant at Kilgobbin, was a Captain in the rebel army and it is believed that a number of the rebel leaders were in Kilgobbin Castle at the time. As the cavalry approached Talbot's men opened fire, killing one of the horsemen and injuring another. Kilgobbin Castle was taken.

The precise extent of the battle at Kilgobbin is not known and probably never will be, but local tradition has it that a field to the north of the castle, now part of the Sandyford Hall development, is called the battlefield, and cannon balls are said to have been dug up from time to time. This suggests something more than a brief exchange of musket fire, and possibly even a skirmish outside the defences of the castle.

In the following month, a force of Wicklow rebels moved on Dublin. A regiment of government forces marched out to meet them and defeated them at Deansgrange. Reports put the size of the rebel forces at a thousand men, with between sixty and a hundred killed, while the government troops claim to have lost only one man wounded. The rebels fell back on Carrickmines

Castle, which was their stronghold in south Dublin.

In late March 1642, a government force laid siege on Carrickmines Castle. Precise details of the casualties on both sides vary, but it would seem that the government forces were not so lucky as they had been at Deansgrange. The official account lists seven government soldiers killed and nine wounded, while another states that forty died. Both of these accounts relate that the besiegers then massacred the occupants of Carrickmines Castle, amounting to between two hundred and three hundred and fifty people. There is another contemporary account, however, that claims that there were only fifteen rebels in Carrickmines Castle and that they killed five hundred government troops before escaping with a loss of only two of their own men.

Whichever of these accounts is correct, three facts are not disputed. Firstly, amongst those killed at Carrickmines was Sir Simon Harcourt, one of the principal leaders of the government forces seeking to quell the rebellion. Secondly, all accounts agree that some hundreds of people were killed, with only disagreement as to which side suffered the casualties. Thirdly, and with the greatest long term effect on the district, Carrickmines Castle was razed to the ground, leaving only a fragment of a gate house standing. As we saw earlier, traces of the extensive earthworks in the vicinity of the castle show something of the size and location of this once-important castle.

The rebellion in south County Dublin was effectively over at this stage. Kilgobbin Castle was held by government forces for a time, and a list of garrisons in the Marquis of Ormonde's regiment in August 1642 included Lehaunstown and Kilgobbin, under the command of Colonel Monck. In July of the following year, there is a report that Ormonde, as Lieutenant General, ordered Captain William Parsons to march with his horse troop to Kilgobbin.

It was a considerable time before the rebellion was over throughout Ireland, and it was finally stamped out with some ferocity following Cromwell's arrival in August 1649, though even then it was another year before it was finally quelled. Thus this bitter conflict ended in as bloody a way as it had started. In the aftermath a great many of the local castles along with their lands were confiscated due to their owners' involvement in the rebellion. In view of the political, rather than purely religious, dimension to the conflict, quite a number of these people had their property restored to them following the death of Cromwell and the subsequent restoration of the monarchy. The confiscation of property was based on the *Civil Survey* which was carried out in 1654. The table of that survey relating to Kilgobbin is shown in Figure 6.

In the case of Kilgobbin, however, the Walsh family was no longer in occupation by the time of the rebellion, and the Civil Survey shows us that the new owner had been Sir Adam Loftus of Rathfarnham. As he lived at Rathfarnham Castle he did not occupy Kilgobbin in person, but had it let to a tenant. It is ironic that this tenant, Matthew Talbot, proved to be so heavily involved in the rebellion, as Sir Adam Loftus was commander of a troop of horse during the uprising, and was involved in the attempts to crush it.

The Census of 1659

There was a census in 1659 and while it was not accurate by modern standards, something may be gleaned from it. That census lists the number of people at each place, notes how many were "English" and how many "Irish" and gives the names of the principal occupiers. The division into English and Irish was a political definition, given the troubles of the time, this being during the time of the English puritan parliament, shortly after the death of Cromwell, when the exact nature of the future government of these islands was still undecided and the political system was unstable.

The places listed in the census correspond with the townlands, though these are not the same townlands as exist now, but tend to be larger and fewer. Kilgobbin townland at that time included the entire area of the modern townlands of Kilgobbin, Woodside, Newtown Little, Ballyedmonduff, Ballybrack (near Glencullen) and Barnacullia. Most of that area was sparsely occupied and the inhabitants listed would have lived predominantly at Kilgobbin. The only other townland in Kilgobbin parish is Jamestown and this was listed separately in the census of 1659. The numbers of people listed in that census may refer to the numbers of households, so that to get a full picture of the size of the population the figure should be multiplied by some factor.

The number of people stated to be in Kilgobbin in 1659 was 37, consisting of 27 English and 10 Irish. The principal occupiers were stated to be Dr John Harding, Anthony Straughton and William Straughton his son. In comparison with other parts of the district which we shall take as the area between Rathfarnham and the Bray river, the population of Kilgobbin was not large. It was the same as that of Ballyman, which today contains very

The parish of KILLGOBBIN, with its bounds, &c.

The said parish of Killgobbin is bounded on the East with the parish of Tully, on the South with the parish of Kilternan, on the West with the parish of Tannee, and on the North with the parish of Kill.

Proprietors names and qualifications.	Denominations of Lands.	Number of acres by estimate of the country.	Land profitable, and its quantity.	Land unprofitable and waste.	Value of the whole and each of the said lands, as it was in 1640.
Sir Adam Loftus of Rathfarnham. Knt. English Protestant.	Jamestown and Killgobbin, by estimate four plow-lands.	Seven hundred acres.	A. R. P. Meadow - 20 0 0 Arable - 200 0 0 Rocky } 480 0 0 Pasture		By the jury two hundred and forty pounds. By us two hundred and eighty pounds.

OBSERVATIONS.

To the proprietor.
To the buildings, &c.

To the woods, &c.
To the royalties, tythes, &c.
To the bounds,

The proprietor was possessed of the premises as his inheritance, and mortgaged the same to Sir Maurice Eustace, Knt. There are on the premises one castle thatched, and a garden-plot, and the walls of a parish church; the said buildings are valued at twenty pounds by the jury.
There are on the premises eight acres of shrubby wood.
The tythes did belong to the College of Dublin.
The premises are bounded on the East with Carrickmaine, on the South with Glannemuck, on the West with Ballawly, and on the North with Mollianltown,

The whole number of acres contained in the said parish of Killgobbin, is as followeth,

	A. R. P.
Meadow -	20 0 0
Arable -	200 0 0
Pasture -	480 0 0
in all	700 0 0

Seven hundred acres.

Figure 6. The Civil Survey of 1654: Table relating to Kilgobbin

few houses and no recognisable centre. Kilgobbin's population was roughly the same as Booterstown, Stillorgan and Shankill, a little less than Dundrum and a little more than Little Bray, Roebuck and Cornelscourt. Places with substantially greater populations included Shanganagh, Old Connaught, Carrickmines, Loughlinstown, Monkstown, Deansgrange, and, largest of all, Bullock.

What is noticeable about Kilgobbin is that it is the only place in that entire district that lists three principal occupiers. Only Stillorgan lists two, while most places had none mentioned at all. Whether this has any significance for the importance of Kilgobbin would be hard to say. The other point to emerge from the census is that Kilgobbin and Jamestown were virtually the only places that had significantly more English residents than Irish. On average the Irish population outnumbered the English by four to one, while in Kilgobbin the proportions are almost reversed, with 27 English to 10 Irish in Kilgobbin and 18 English to 3 Irish in Jamestown. This statistic also seems difficult to interpret. Five years before, the Civil Survey of 1654 had found that of eleven parishes in the Dublin part of Rathdown barony, in eight of them the majority of land was held by "Irish Papist" proprietors. In Donnybrook the land was divided fairly evenly between the Irish and English, while only in Kilgobbin and Whitechurch was no land at all held by Catholics.

It is worth commenting that in 1841 the population of Jamestown was less than the 21 persons listed in 1659, and for much of the nineteenth century it was not much more. The 1659 census listed 18 persons at both Murphystown and Balally, and in both cases this was split into 7 English and 11 Irish. In neither case is the occupier named. Carrickmines was somewhat more populous with 59 persons, 5 of whom were English and 54 Irish.

The late 17th Century

As we have seen, Kilgobbin Castle was owned by Sir Adam Loftus during the rebellion and occupied by one of the rebels, Matthew Talbot. We have also seen that the census of 1659 listed three new names as occupiers of Kilgobbin. The Civil Survey of 1654 had listed the castle, a garden and the ruins of the church and gave a valuation of £20 on the buildings at Kilgobbin and a valuation of between £240 and £280 on the townland.

Dr Harding was an Englishman who had been brought to Ireland in 1636 to a position as fellow of Trinity College, Dublin on account of his being an ardent monarchist. In 1637 he was Vice-Provost of the College and from 1639 to 1643 he was Chancellor of Christ Church. In the turbulent 1640's he became a supporter of the Commonwealth just as vehemently as he had been ^ Royalist beforehand, for which he was imprisoned and deported back to ɔngland. He returned to Ireland with Cromwell's army and after the rebellion was crushed he returned to the college. He was in Kilgobbin by 1659 and died there in 1664 or 1665.

According to The O'Murchoe's *History of Kilternan and Kilgobbin* the Straughtons listed in the Census of 1659 were evidently the Staughton family who afterwards settled in Kerry.

In the ensuing years the Kilgobbin area settled down into a pattern of stability in which the principal occupation was agriculture and the land became occupied by a number of separate farms, the boundaries of which have strongly influenced the land holdings which exist today. We will consider these further in a later section, as the late seventeenth century occupation of the land is pertinent in looking at the early eighteenth century.

7. THE CHURCH OF IRELAND

The Reformation in the mid-16th century created a strange anomaly in Ireland. Under the system introduced following the Norman invasion the Church was an integral part of the organisation of the State. Even into the second half of the 19th century this remained the case and the relief of poverty, for instance, was the responsibility of the parish, as we know from *Oliver Twist*, hence the term *on the parish*, meaning being in receipt of poor relief. In fact, the parish had quite a number of other duties that survived into that century and expressions like *the parish pump* testify to this. In medieval times, the church had an even more obvious responsibility in functions such as justice, and the archbishop held periodic courts in a range of places such as Swords, Tallaght and Shankill. On a national level, the administration of the law relating to wills and the granting of probate was the responsibility of the ecclesiastical courts.

When Henry VIII broke from the Church of Rome and declared himself to be the head of the Church of England it followed, naturally, that the various functions of the pre-Reformation church would continue to be performed by the new Anglican church. This has continued to be the case in England where the Church of England remains, to this day, part of the State, with the reigning monarch as titular head, and the church has a status that is taken for granted in English life. While the original non-religious functions of the church have mostly been replaced by local government, the National Health Service, the judiciary and so forth, some of them remain, such as the entitlement of Church of England bishops to a seat in the House of Lords.

Henry VIII was also king of Ireland and there was no reason why the Anglican church should not assume the same functions in Ireland as it had in England. At the time no-one could have predicted that the population at large would not follow the change in circumstances and that the new Established Church of Ireland would remain the church of a minority of the populace. Even if it had been possible to predict this outcome, it is difficult to see what could have been done about it. In later years there were attempts to coerce the people into abandoning Catholicism, but even if there had been a more tolerant attitude it is hard to see, in the circumstances of the time, how a monarch that was head of the church could have presided over a country where many of the functions of state were run by a different church.

In essence, the problem of the Reformation was that it was not just a matter of differences of belief, but that the church was so heavily involved in government and administration.

Post-Reformation Decline

What was a religious anomaly in theory became a paradox in practice, as the existing church buildings came under the wing of the established Church of Ireland with few adherents, while the majority of the population had no places of worship. One result was that a number of churches went out of use, while others deteriorated through neglect. The date when many of these churches went out of use is unknown, including Jamestown, and some may even have been disused before the Reformation. Some that were not parish churches, such as Ballyman, near Bray, seem to have gone into immediate disuse at the Reformation

In other cases, churches managed to struggle on for quite a number of years. This is understandable, as a building that starts off in reasonable condition will keep going without attention for quite a while before becoming derelict or ruinous. By 1609, the strain was beginning to tell, and an order was issued requiring the parishioners of a number of parish churches to repair the walls and roofs. The list included Tully, Kilgobbin and Taney. In 1615, three generations after the Reformation, a survey was taken of the churches and found that of more than twenty churches in the area between Rathfarnham and Bray only about half a dozen were in good repair. Amongst those in ruins were Kilternan and Kilgobbin. This suggests that by 1609 Kilternan was already considered to be not worth repairing, or it would have appeared on the list of churches needing attention. It also shows that despite the inclusion of Kilgobbin in the list in 1609, nothing seems to have been done and the church fell into disrepair. The Civil Survey of 1654 states that at Kilgobbin there were "the walls of a parish church". Taney was in good repair in 1615 and must have heeded the call for repairs six years previously. Fifteen years later, however, Taney, along with others that had been in good condition in 1615, was found to be ruinous.

Thus, a hundred years after the Reformation the number of Church of Ireland churches in this area had fallen to a mere handful. Stillorgan was in poor condition, but was repaired and soldiered on to become the oldest continuously-used church site in south-east County Dublin. Rathmichael and

Tully were in use in 1630, but in both cases the chancels were in ruins and neither church lasted much longer. Kill of the Grange was suffering from storm damage in 1630, and also went out of use not many years later as also did Whitechurch. It is not known when the church at Balally went out of use, though it will be looked at later when we consider the Roman Catholic church.

Recovery

Exactly which church has the distinction of being the first Anglican church to be built in Ireland after the Reformation will probably never be known. We do know that a new archbishop was appointed to the Anglican See of Dublin in 1702 and, like the proverbial new broom, he set about improving the state of churches in the diocese. Kilgobbin was one of the churches that he ordered to be rebuilt, and the new building was in use by 1707. Samuel Lewis, in his *Topographical Dictionary of Ireland,* published in 1837, stated that the church of Kilgobbin was said to have been the first erected after the Reformation. However, he also states that St Paul's Church in Bray was erected in 1609, almost a century before Kilgobbin. Lewis himself cannot be blamed for this inconsistency, as he merely edited information supplied to him from local sources, and we should note that he wrote that Kilgobbin *was said to have been* the first. A search of his entire *Topographical Dictionary* may well reveal other churches around Ireland for which this claim is made. The local inhabitants at Kilgobbin told the Ordnance Survey a similar story in the 1830's. In fact, St Columb's Cathedral in Derry was built between 1628 and 1633, which quite definitely puts paid to any claims by any of the contenders in the Dublin area which are considerably younger than this except, possibly, Bray.

To a large extent the issue of the date of the early churches is confused by the uncertainty about what was newly built and what was merely the repair of an older structure. Bray was one of the churches ordered to be repaired in 1609 and it may be that substantial repairs were carried out. It may also be that the building was in such poor state that it had to be demolished and rebuilt. Similarly, Kilgobbin was an existing church that had been out of use for about a century, and it is not known whether any part of the old walls were incorporated in the new church. It is also worth noting that the old church at Carrickbrennan, or Monkstown, had gone out of use in the middle of the 17th century, but had been rebuilt in 1688. At around the same time that Kilgobbin was rebuilt, Rathfarnham church seems also to reappear after a period of disuse not far short of a century.

Thus, in the early years of the 18th century, Kilgobbin received its new church, not for its sole use, but to serve also the parishes of Taney and Cruagh. Although the Established Church had seen an improvement in its supply of churches, the area between Rathfarnham and the Bray River had only four churches in use: Kilgobbin, Rathfarnham, Stillorgan and Carrickbrennan. A significant section of the Anglican community was served by churches outside this area at Donnybrook and at Bray, and the latter was the church that served Kilternan, despite the proximity of Kilgobbin. Balally and most of Sandyford lay within Taney parish and therefore used Kilgobbin church, while Murphystown was officially under the church at Monkstown. In fact, it seems probable that the occupants of Murphystown used Kilgobbin church because it was nearby.

Later in the eighteenth century, as the population of the area grew, this area only acquired one further Anglican church. The old church at Taney was rebuilt in 1760, and is still with us, now known as St Naithi's to distinguish it from the parish church of Taney, the official name of which is Christ Church, Taney. While this may have meant an increase in the number of churches held by the Church of Ireland, it was not a good thing for the Anglican community at Kilgobbin as it removed a significant proportion of the attenders at Kilgobbin church by splitting Taney parish away from its connections with Kilgobbin.

Decline of Kilgobbin church

The rebuilding of Taney parish church left Kilgobbin out on a limb. If the Anglican churches of south east County Dublin were to be shown on a map it would be seen that the small number of churches were widely spaced and that there were fewer large mansions in the Kilgobbin area than in many other places such as Blackrock, Roebuck, Stillorgan, Dundrum and Old Connaught. These large houses of the gentry tended to have a higher proportion of Anglican occupiers than in the population at large and they were also usually generous benefactors of the churches. However, the picture as seen on a map does not reflect the true position. The parish system was in disarray because so few of the parishes had a church of their own, but the absence of a church in a parish did not automatically place the parish under the wing of the nearest alternative. Each churchless parish was officially united with or joined with a parish that had a church and the way in which this was organised left Kilgobbin isolated. Taney parish extended right up to Sandyford village to include Balally and Ballinteer and now had its own church. Murphystown was in Tully parish and although very close to Kilgobbin and reasonably close to Stillorgan, its official parish church was at Monkstown. Kilternan, as we have noted, was joined to Bray and parishioners had to travel a considerable distance to church rather than to the more convenient Kilgobbin.

This left Kilgobbin serving only its own parish and Kilgobbin was not the most populous parish in the area. Much of the parish was mountain land, and the only settlements were Kilgobbin itself and the embryonic Stepaside, with only the less populous part of Sandyford lying within the parish. Predictably, the circumstances soon affected the fabric of the church which deteriorated and by the early years of the 19th century it seems to have been a fairly miserable building. Anyone who visits the ruins of the old church today would find it hard to envisage services being held in such a confined space.

A booklet produced in 1976 by the parish of Kilternan entitled *Kilternan Church 1826-1976*, paints a vivid picture of the state of Kilgobbin church in the second decade of the 19th century, incorporating two fairly graphic descriptions by people who had known the church in use:

By 1818 (Kilgobbin church) was deemed to be too small and in poor repair. There survive several accounts of Kilgobbin church in the early 19th century. Teresa Moss (Née Richardson) who was born in 1818, recalled in old age that she attended the church when five years old: "We walked up the grassy bank as the bell tolled, swinging in and out through an opening in the spire. The Sextoness, in blue and orange shawl, ran up the bank to open the church door. The choral part of the service depended on the clerk and sextoness, who were also the only school teachers". The Rev. George Bellett (1797-1886), who lived in Kilgobbin as a boy, wrote "Nothing could well be more wretched than old Kilgobbin Church in respect of its appearance and what went on in it. The walls were green with damp, the congregation was very scant, the old clerk singing solo, and from one year's end to another the same psalm 149, to the same tune, Handel's 104th"

In the circumstances, Kilgobbin church would either have to find an injection of new support or it would succumb. What happened was that a new curate took up the appointment to Kilgobbin in 1817 and breathed new life into the parish. Following the arrival of the Rev. Henry Kearney attendance at the church increased to the extent that it was proposed to build a new gallery to accommodate the increase. In 1818 a new glebe house was built on the church lands near to Kilternan and moves started to provide new accommodation for the church. The result was an act of parliament in 1823 which provided for the splitting of Kilternan parish from its union with Bray and the uniting of Kilternan with Kilgobbin in a new parish to be called Kilternan. Recognising that Kilgobbin church was beyond repair, the act provided for the building of a new church. The site of Kilgobbin church is not particularly suitable for a modern parish church, being on a very restricted site on the top of a steep hillock. Presumably this was taken into account in deciding to opt for a new site and the location selected was nearer to the centre of population of the new combined parish. The curate, Rev. Henry Kearney was to be the first incumbent of the new parish, and the existing churchwardens of Kilgobbin were to continue to hold these positions. History does not relate how the inhabitants of Kilternan felt about being excluded from these positions.

No time was lost in organising the new parish. A site was organised by September 1823 and handed over to the churchwardens, John Richardson and John G Bellett. A loan of £500 for the building of the new church was provided by the Board of First Fruits, the body responsible for assisting in the provision of new buildings for the Established Church. This body had previously provided a grant of £450 and a loan of £50 for the building of the glebe house, but it had refused to assist in the repair of Kilgobbin church on the grounds that the repair of churches was outside its area of responsibility. The architect for the church was John Semple, the Board's architect for the Leinster area. He was responsible for a number of churches in the Dublin area at this time and his distinctive style is normally quite evident. The high pointed arch over the main door at Kilternan is very similar to others such as the Black Church in the north of Dublin city and at Monkstown parish church which Semple extended and remodelled. He was also responsible for work at Whitechurch, Rathfarnham and Rathmines and he designed the round room at Dublin's mansion house.

The new Kilternan parish church was ready for worship in 1826. The parishioners of the former parish of Kilgobbin were prominent amongst the congregation of the new church and included Alderman Darley of Fernhill, George F Mowlds of Larkfield, John Hastings of Woodside, Mr Warren of St Patrick's Well and John Richardson, William Shea and Mrs Cuthbert of Kilgobbin.

The disused church

The old church at Kilgobbin was abandoned and before long it was unroofed. There is a suggestion that the church continued for a time to be used for other purposes. Even when a Church of Ireland parish was redefined, as had happened here, the old parish boundaries were still retained for administrative purposes and continued to the end of the nineteenth century as an administrative unit. The old Kilgobbin parish had its own commissioners to assess the tithes, which was the tax levied to provide funds for the Established Church. In October 1828 these Commissioners certified that they had "attended at the church of Kilgobbin on Thursday the 31st day of July last ..... to hear and decide objections, if any, to the valuation and estimate for said parish". However, the reference to the church of Kilgobbin may have meant the new church at Kilternan which, after all, was serving Kilgobbin parish. That this is the case is suggested by a notice of a special vestry meeting in the previous year which was "held in the Parish Church of Kilgobbin .... 16th October 1827 for the purpose of taking into consideration ..... the certificate of commissioners (which was published) in said parish church and on the old church and Roman Catholic Chapels in said parish". The context here suggests that if the notice was posted on the parish church and the old church then the parish church referred to must be the new one. The plural chapels supports this, as one of the chapels was in the former Kilternan parish, not Kilgobbin. This seems to be a case that the occupants of the former Kilgobbin parish had not come to terms with the parish church being in Kilternan rather than Kilgobbin, and they continued to refer to the new parish as Kilgobbin. In any event, the old church was certainly in ruins by 1838 when the historian John D'Alton referred to "the ruins of the church".

The ruin of the old church and the churchyard remained in the hands of the parish of Kilternan until the disestablishment of the Church of Ireland in 1869. This was when the Church of Ireland ceased to be the official church of the state, analogous to being privatised. One of the features of disestablishment was to take from the church any property that was not in active use for the purposes for which the church existed such as public worship and education. This was a double edged sword as it took from the church property that was providing an income but it also removed the responsibility for maintaining property that was not profitable and may even have been a liability. Property that was considered to be of national archaeological importance, such as Glendalough and Cashel, was vested in the Office of Public Works, as the department of state responsible for property, and that Office retains responsibility for archaeology to this day.

Burial grounds that were not attached to churches in use were handed over to the health authorities. At the time the Board of Guardians of the Rathdown Union was the health authority for the area which included Kilgobbin and its health functions were later taken over by the Board of Public Health. This function is now looked after by the County Council and the council maintains Kilgobbin's old churchyard. The old graveyard was closed for burials by Ministerial Order in 1905 and the new cemetery was opened in the 1920's. It is also now closed, except for those with burial rights.

It is worth noting that the Reformation did not affect burial and the old churchyards throughout Ireland continued to be used by the entire population regardless of creed, though often with stipulations that only Church of Ireland clergy were permitted to officiate. It was only later, when the two denominations built new churches in the early nineteenth century, that the burials were divided on religious grounds, such as at the new Church of Ireland parish church at Kilternan and the Roman Catholic church at Glencullen. In the nineteenth century specifically Catholic cemeteries were established such as Goldenbridge and Glasnevin, to overcome the problem of the exclusion of Catholic priests from funeral services, though non-Catholics were not excluded from these cemeteries. A little later, public authorities started to set up non-denominational cemeteries such as Deansgrange, which was established by the Board of Guardians of the Rathdown Union in the 1860's.

Multi-denominational burials continued at Kilgobbin and after the closure of the church it became possible to erect larger monuments within its walls. It is curious that the only memorial stone within the church that relates to a burial while the church was still in use is in memory of Thomas Callaghan, who was a Catholic. This slab was moved in to the church later so that Thomas Callaghan is not actually buried on that spot. After the church became disused the earliest memorial in the church is to the Strong family of Glenamuck, the earliest burial recorded on which is 1831. It is probable that the church was unroofed by this time as prominent parishioners are unlikely to have sought burials within a derelict building with a collapsing roof. Elizabeth Kearney, wife of the Rector of Kilternan, was buried within the church in 1834 and her husband followed in 1855. The other two memorials are to the Bayly family and the Cuthbert sisters, all of whom lived in the heart of Kilgobbin.

The whereabouts of the burial records for Kilgobbin is unknown. The Church of Ireland's parish records go back to 1817, but where earlier records have gone to is a mystery. The Rev O Murchoe wrote earlier in this century that the parish registers before that date were probably entered in the registers of St Peter's, Dublin, but a search of those records has failed to trace a connection. Records for the Catholic parish of Sandyford and Glencullen exist only from 1856, but these refer to births and marriages rather than deaths.

8.   THE ROMAN CATHOLIC CHURCH

Whatever chaos the Established Church may have been in following the Reformation was minor compared with the circumstances pertaining in the Catholic church. It found itself without any churches or other property, no hierarchy or other organisation and no funds or other resources except its congregation and those of the priests who, like their flock, did not switch to the new church.

Contrary to popular belief, the religious divide was not simply on the basis of wealth, nor whether one's ancestors were of Gaelic or English origin. In this, our area was fortunate, as the Walsh family, who occupied the castles at Kilgobbin, Balally and Carrickmines and were the landholders, retained the Catholic faith. They were not alone, and their Walsh kinsmen elsewhere in the vicinity also remained Catholic, including those at Brenanstown, Shanganagh and Old Connaught. Other landholders in the vicinity that held to the old faith included the Lawlesses at Shankill and the Goodmans of Loughlinstown. In various other places, if the landowners were not Catholics at the outset, the property soon came into Catholic hands, as at Bullock, Monkstown and Cornelscourt. In effect, much of south east County Dublin was in Catholic hands by the early 17th century.

The result of this was that while the older churches had been absorbed into the new established church along with the means of support for the clergy, the wealthier landowners of south east Dublin tended to retain the services of a priest who would often minister to the needs of the population at large. At Old Connaught, James Walsh went further and is reported as maintaining several priests and friars. Mass was celebrated regularly at the Walsh property at Balally. It is not known when the old church of Balally went out of use, but it has been suggested that it may have been the venue for Catholic services in the 17th century. Archbishop Bulkeley reported in 1650 that a priest called Cahill commonly said Mass there. It is also likely that the Walsh castle was the location for the celebration of the Mass, just as in Walsh castles in other areas. At Carrickmines, Theobald Walsh maintained a priest, Turlough Reilly, and a friar, Patrick Comin, who celebrated mass in his mansion house and which was attended by the populace of the surrounding area publicly. Given their actions in other areas, it is quite possible that the Walshes maintained a priest at Kilgobbin, though there is no information to prove this either way.

It was not until 1615, about three generations after the Reformation, that the Catholic church recovered sufficiently to re-establish some kind of territorial organisation. Given the lack of resources, both in finances and manpower, no attempt was made to follow the old parish divisions. In fact, the new areas were vastly larger. Our area found itself in a new parish that stretched from Dundrum to Bray and from Three Rock to the sea. At a time when most parishioners had no transport other than by foot, this area was huge.

At first, the new parish was based in a converted house in Monkstown, but later in the 17th century a more central location was chosen at Cabinteely. The parish priest lived at Loughlinstown in the 18th and early 19th centuries and the parish was normally known as the parish of Loughlinstown. The sheer size of this area meant that it could not be cared for by a single parish priest and curates were appointed to look after the areas around Kilternan and Old Connaught.

Precise information about where and when Catholic churches were built is not available due to the almost overwhelming difficulties of running a church that was not lawful and for which full records could not usually be kept. Where records were made, circumstances did not favour their survival. The penal laws were not evenly enforced and while the early to mid eighteenth century was a time of particularly strong anti-Catholic laws, this is also the time when the first solid evidence appears for Catholic churches in this area. The precise location of the churches at Cabinteely and Old Connaught in the middle of the 18th century is known, but the one at Kilternan is less clear. In all likelihood this was the mass shelter at Newtown, Glencullen which seems to have been built by 1737. There was also a chapel or mass shelter at Sandyford, close to the present Church. Its date can only be guessed at, but there seems to have been some form of chapel here by at least 1731. In that year it was reported that there was a priest at Kilgobbin. At that time Sandyford had not established a separate identity from Kilgobbin, and was generally taken that the lands of Kilgobbin included Woodside and stretched as far as Sandyford. It is probable that this priest was based at Sandyford rather than the town of Kilgobbin, as some years later, in 1779, it is clear that the priest at that time, a Rev. James Mulvey, lived at "Sandyford, near Kilgobbin". In May of that year he suffered a vicious attack by a group of intruders who stole property and slashed the priest with a knife. There is a report, however, that Mass was celebrated in Kilgobbin Castle at a time when an old man had converted part of the ruin into a dwelling for himself. The context suggests that this was in the mid-18th century, and it may be that there was a priest in residence locally at that time and possibly this was in 1731.

In the early 19th century there was a significant number of Catholic chapels in the south east Dublin area. Taylor's map of *The Environs of Dublin*, published in 1816, marks chapels at Booterstown, Blackrock, Crinken, Cabinteely, Cornelscourt, Newtown (Glencullen), Sandyford, Dundrum and Rathfarnham. It is commonly believed that there were no Catholic churches until Catholic Emancipation in 1829. In fact, the lifting of the penal laws started in the 1770's and almost all had gone by the early 1790's. By then Catholics could vote, enter professions, study at Trinity College, own land, build churches and so forth. The only bar that remained until 1829 was the right to sit in parliament and it was this that O'Connell achieved under the title Catholic Emancipation for which he traded the right of many Catholics and others to vote at all! The main impediment to Catholic church building in the early nineteenth century was finance, but this problem was gradually overcome.

Early in the 19th century both the Anglican church and the Catholic church began to build substantial new churches throughout south County Dublin. The first major new Catholic church to be completed in the area was St Patrick's at Glencullen, built in 1824 with financial assistance from the Fitzsimon family. The construction of St Mary's church at Sandyford started in about 1807, to replace the old chapel which was in such poor condition that it was in danger of being destroyed by the wind, but due to lack of funds the new church was not in use until 1830. As mentioned, Taylor's map marks a chapel at Sandyford (Figure 10) and it is likely that this refers to the old chapel, often referred to as a mass shelter, rather than to the new one under construction. The date of 1830 normally given for the completion of the new church also begs the question as to what constitutes completion. It probably refers to its being ready for use rather than being totally complete, as Samuel Lewis, in his *Topographical Dictionary of Ireland*, published in 1837, wrote that the chapel at Sandyford was "a spacious building, which, though commenced twenty years since, is not yet finished". Even later than this, Thom's Directory in 1848 stated that "at Sandyford there is a large but unfinished Roman Catholic Chapel".

The huge parish of Loughlinstown was split into two separate parishes in

1829, when Sandyford became a parish in its own right, including Kilgobbin, Kilternan and Glencullen. This created a remarkable situation whereby Sandyford parish had two churches serving a population of not much more than two thousand, while the remaining section of the parish, now based at Kingstown, had three churches serving a population of over seventeen thousand. The creation of the new Sandyford parish reflected the reality that this part of Loughlinstown parish had functioned as a separate parish in all but in name for a considerable period.

9. LANDLORDS AND TENANTS

One of the best known aspects of Irish history in the 19th century is the land question - an issue which features in the stories of the Great Famine, the evictions of tenants and the land war which accompanied the rise of Parnell. However the issue of landlordism is frequently greatly over-simplified into a division of society into wealthy, powerful landlords and poverty stricken, powerless tenants. In reality the picture was far more complicated. The landlords mentioned in history were often not the head landlords, but tenants in a chain of leases. The rent paid by the occupier of the land may have had to be divided between a string of people with some kind of interest in the land. To add to this, many of the landlords had various financial commitments to meet out of the income of their estates. The result was a system of land tenure that was based on a fairly simple concept of landlord and tenant, but which had become fairly complicated even by the 17th century.

The increase in population in the 18th century put pressure on land, allowing rents to increase and fuelling the problems as tenants sublet their property to help meet the rent and their tenants, in turn, sublet to lesser tenants. At the same time the landlords would frequently have to pay fixed charges out of the income of their land to support a widening circle of relatives and this encouraged further subletting. As the population boomed in the 19th century the problem became virtually out of control. Many landowners found themselves so deep in debt that they need to sell their property, but the estate would be so encumbered with mortgages, financial charges and so forth that it was impossible to sell it. The problem peaked in the 1840's as a result of the large numbers of landlords ruined by the economic effects of the Famine. To overcome this deadlock the first of the major land reforms was introduced in 1849. Gradually, over the next sixty years, several land acts were brought in, spurred by political agitation by Michael Davitt, Charles Stewart Parnell and others. By the early years of the twentieth century, the old landlord system had effectively been dismantled.

Over the next few pages a summary is given of the principal landowners in our area between about 1700 and 1850. Not all of the landowners are included, as some of them held only small amounts of land, or for only a short time. In general the list includes the landowners higher up the chain of landlords and tenants and only a few of the actual occupiers of land appear.

Many of the characters appearing in this section are lesser or middle gentry and professional people and their families. It should be remembered that at that time land was one the principal means of investment. There were no pension funds and life insurance policies only became common later on. A gentleman could therefore only ensure an income for the future by investment. This was most commonly in property, and this would have been the reason why most of these people acquired interests in lands in our area while not occupying the land. Landlords whose lands were let on long leases had a perpetual income from the property and could use their interest for raising loans or, alternatively, the land could be treated as an asset when the debts were called in. Mortgages were frequently raised on property and there were also *rent charges* or *annuities* on the land. These were legally binding agreements to provide a certain annual sum to someone out of the rental income of the property. Often these resulted from *marriage settlements*. When a marriage was arranged the families would come to an agreement to hand capital over to trustees for the benefit of the marriage. This would be used to ensure that the wife and children of the marriage were provided for to safeguard them in the event of the death of the husband and also to ensure that he could not abandon them leaving them unsupported.

In the following accounts two things should be borne in mind. Firstly, unless specifically stated, the acres which are mentioned are *Irish acres* or *Irish plantation acres,* which were substantially larger than the statute acre, being equivalent to more than 1.6 statute acres. These remained the official measure of land in Ireland until the 1830's when the Ordnance Survey adopted the statute acre for its work. Even then, the Irish acre continued to be used even up to the present day in some documents, just as the statute acre continues to be used now, ten years after it has been replaced by the metric system. Secondly, the spelling of names did not become standardised until the nineteenth century. Where variations on the spelling of a name were possible they usually occurred. To some extent the spelling of one individual's name may remain constant while someone else in the family has a consistently different spelling. In the descriptions below the spelling adopted is that which was normally found for a particular individual. This leads to some apparent inconsistency such as the O'Rourkes of Jamestown who, when they first appear are either Rourke or Rorke, while later they become O'Rourke or, sometimes, O'Rorke. There are cases when husband

and wife have different spellings, such as Edytha Baldwin widow of Arthur Baldwyn.

The Loftus and Conolly families

The land tenure at Kilgobbin was no less complicated than in other parts of the country and, as in other cases, it is frequently difficult to disentangle the hierarchy of land tenure. The Walsh family, who had built Kilgobbin Castle, had been the landowners at Kilgobbin until the mid 17th century, when Sir Adam Loftus acquired the land. It is not known exactly when or how he came into possession, but the Civil Survey of 1654 stated that he "was possessed of the premises as his inheritance". It is probable that this refers to the land being part of the family estate rather than his own personal property, and not that he inherited it. The Civil Survey also states that Sir Adam had mortgaged Kilgobbin to Sir Maurice Eustace which is not surprising, as the Loftus family had suffered heavy financial losses in the wars of the 1640's and was reduced to poverty, Sir Adam himself being imprisoned for debt.

The Loftus family never occupied Kilgobbin, but were based at Rathfarnham where Sir Adam's grandfather had built Rathfarnham Castle in the 1580's. Their landed estate was enormous, taking in huge amounts of County Dublin around Rathfarnham and to the south and west. Rathfarnham had previously been occupied by the Eustace family and they still maintained some involvement in the property. Apart from the mortgage which Sir Maurice Eustace held in the 1650's, he was also the grantor of leases at Kilgobbin in the 1690's and it would appear that he held the Kilgobbin land as a tenant of the Loftus family. However, that is the last time the Eustace family appears in connection with Kilgobbin, while the link with the Rathfarnham estate continued. The Loftus family's descendants sold the estate in the 1720's and it was acquired subsequently by Thomas Conolly, Speaker of the Irish House of Commons. Conolly was an enormously successful man and acquired great wealth. Perhaps his finest legacy was the building of Castletown House, near Celbridge. The Conolly family remained the head landlords at Kilgobbin for many generations, but they had no direct involvement with the area as it was all subject to long term leases. The Loftus family, and after them the Conollys, owned the entire parish of Kilgobbin, including the mountain area at Ballybrack, near Glencullen. The source of fuel for households in many parts of Ireland became a problem as the native forests grew smaller and smaller and there was no indigenous coal. Turf was the fuel wherever it was available, and within the parish of Kilgobbin it was available in Ballybrack. The leases granted by the Loftus family and the subsidiary leases granted by all the middle landlords included a permission for the tenant to gather turf from Ballybrack for their own personal use, though this would not have extended to cutting it for sale in the city.

The Baldwin and Bayly families

We have already seen how Sir Maurice Eustace seems to have held the lands of Kilgobbin as a tenant of Sir Adam Loftus. He, in turn, let it to tenants. At least as early as 1739 the Eustace lease had come into the possession of the Baldwin family. The Baldwins lived at Redcross, Co Wicklow where they held a significant amount of land as well as other land in Wicklow town, Dublin city and north County Dublin. At the end of the eighteenth century, however, the family was represented by Charles Baldwin who ran into cash flow difficulties and sold the Kilgobbin property, presumably to meet the various financial obligations.

The purchaser of the lands at Kilgobbin was Emanuel Bayly who paid £6,812-10s for lands which included the townlands which are known today as Kilgobbin, Jamestown, Newtown Little, Woodside, Barnacullia, Ballyedmonduff and Ballybrack. All of this was subject to leases to subtenants and so none of it was available for occupation by Emanuel Bayly. He lived at Dublin and also lived for a time at Bath, though, as we shall see, his grandson later came to live at Kilgobbin.

Thomas Jones

The next link in the chain of land tenure was Thomas Jones, a brewer from Dublin, who took a lease of the lands of Kilgobbin in 1697 from Sir Maurice Eustace. The lands in his lease included not just Kilgobbin itself but also the surrounding lands of the parish of Kilgobbin such as Jamestown, Woodside and Sandyford. Thomas Jones took the lease for investment purposes rather than with any intention of occupying the land himself. Instead, from 1698, he granted leases of individual sections of the lands to various subtenants. This should not be thought of as breaking up a single landholding into smaller sections, as the various sections had been separate tenancies in the

17th century.

It may be helpful to illustrate the hierarchy of tenancies which we have met so far by means of a diagram:

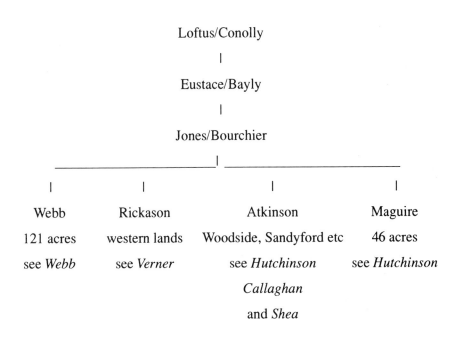

Figure 7: Hierarchy of tenancies: Early 18th century

This shows how Adam Loftus and later the Conolly family were the head landlords of the parish of Kilgobbin and that they leased the entire property to Sir Maurice Eustace, whose interest became the property of the Bayly family. This Sir Maurice, in turn, leased all of the townland of Kilgobbin to Thomas Jones who let it out to separate tenants. The four major landholdings are listed in the final line, but it must be borne in mind that there were other, smaller, plots of land in addition to these. The smaller plots were not insignificant, as will become evident later, as they included the properties in the town of Kilgobbin.

Thomas Jones's interest in the lands at Kilgobbin did not last long into the 18th century and it came into the hands of Christopher Taylor, a gentleman from Dublin. Following Christopher Taylor's death the lease was sold in 1723 to Richard Nutley, a court judge. He granted leases on his property such as 115 acres he let to John Dawson at St Patrick's Well in 1725. By 1730, Richard Nutley had died though his executors continued to grant new leases.

The leases on land in Kilgobbin were sufficiently long that the successors in title of Richard Nutley and the Eyre family more or less disappear into oblivion at this stage. They re-emerge in 1816, however, when Elizabeth Bourchier appeared as the inheritor of the estate. She died in about 1850 and left her interest in the property to her children. They held on to the property through the 1850's, a time when the new land acts had allowed stronger leases to be taken by long term tenants, and as a result fee farm grants were executed to the various sub tenants before 1859 when the family owners ran into financial problems and sold their interest in the property through the Landed Estates Court.

The Verner family

One of the leases from Thomas Jones at the end of the 17th century was to James Rickason, a farmer from Dundrum. He later lived at Ballinteer where he had a substantial amount of land as well as owning property in Dublin city on which he built several houses, and a further piece of land in Dolphin's Barn. The land he held at Kilgobbin included the townlands of Newtown Little and Ballyedmonduff as well as the western portion of the townland of Kilgobbin. This latter section consisted of most of the land west of Stepaside Hill and Kilgobbin Road except for the immediate vicinity of Kilgobbin Castle and Kilgobbin town. James Rickason died in 1721, and his lands in the Kilgobbin area were sold in the following year to John Kerr for £700. In 1749 John Kerr's widow sold the land to Thomas Verner.

The Verner family came from Co Armagh and successive members of the family were Members of Parliament for that county over the years. In 1846,

William Verner was created a baronet. The Verners did not occupy their land here directly, but let it to tenants. Early in the nineteenth century the bulk of the land within Kilgobbin townland was let to John Rorke and later it was leased to John Richardson. The lands at Newtown Little and some of the surrounding parts were leased to Alderman Darley of Fern Hill who also acted as local land agent for the Verners.

The Webb Family

Edward Webb was one of the earliest farmers at Kilgobbin for whom we have significant details of a family history. He took a lease of 121 acres from Thomas Jones in February 1698, consisting of the block of land now occupied by Clay Farm and Kilgobbin Cottage and including eastwards from where Stepaside now stands to the river over towards Ballyogan Road. The 121 acres were in Irish plantation measure, and would be equivalent to 196 statute acres, or 80 hectares.

In the seventeenth century, before he took his lease, the land had been occupied as three separate farms. Now, however, it was merged into a single working farm which was inherited by Edward's son, William Webb by the late 1720's. His house was somewhere in the vicinity of the present Kilgobbin Cottage, and this may also have been his parents' house.

Later in the eighteenth century the Webbs started to run into financial difficulties and this was probably the reason that they started to dispose of their land by way of leases. Over a thirty year period they leased an increasing amount of land to David Fitzgerald, a Dublin surgeon, consisting, by 1800, of some 48 Irish acres. In 1791, almost 30 acres was leased to Edmund Rourke who had leases on adjoining land in Jamestown. Between David Fitzgerald, Edmund Rourke and Eaton Cotter all of the Webb lands here had been let to tenants by 1809.

The Webb family finances had not recovered, despite the injection of funds resulting from these leases, including, for instance, £1,000 from Eaton Cotter. William Webb died in about 1817, leaving a young family of five children, all under 21 years of age. His son and heir, another Edward Webb, was only twelve years old. As a result of the financial difficulties of William Webb's estate the property at Kilgobbin was sold by the High Court of Chancery on behalf of the children.

The Lawless family

The buyer of the Webb lands was Barry Edmund Lawless. He had married Jane Magdelin Byrne in 1814 and the marriage settlement had provided £3,000 to be invested for the benefit of the marriage. Barry Edmund Lawless added some of his own funds to make up the £3,560 that he paid for the 121 acres at Kilgobbin. These were Irish plantation acres, of course, being equivalent to 196 statute acres or 80 hectares, and the land was not available for occupation as the tenancies were still held by Eaton Cotter, David Fitzgerald and John Rorke, son of Edmund Rourke. Over the ensuing years much of the land continued to be let to tenants, and a significant amount of it was taken by the Richardson family. Some of the property came back into the hands of the Lawless family and the family has continued to hold land at Kilgobbin to the present day.

The Hutchinson and O'Neill families

Between 1722 and 1731, John Dawson acquired various leasehold interests in land at Kilgobbin and at Jamestown. He was a hosier from Dublin and his purpose was investment rather than to use the land himself. He therefore let the lands at Kilgobbin and Jamestown to tenants. Following John Dawson's death, his property was acquired by his daughter, Esther, and her husband John Hutchinson. John and Esther Hutchinson had six daughters and no sons. It was quite normal at that time for the bulk of a family's property to be passed on to the eldest son, while a portion of it would be divided equally amongst the other children. Where there were no sons the estate would often be split equally between the daughters. The usual method was to keep the property intact, but to divide the income from it amongst the heirs.

In fact, when the Hutchinson daughters and another party finally came into their inheritance they decided that they did not want to work to this system. Instead, they decided to carve up the ownership between the seven of them and each would be sole owner of her or his own section. Exactly why they decided to do this is unknown, but the most likely explanation is that they could foresee disagreements over the terms of the leases that they might grant. They may even have been forced into it as a result of a court action taken by one of them in July 1797, following which they signed a legal agreement to split up the property. The entire family holding extended to more than 350 plantation acres, equivalent to more than 560 statute acres or 225 hectares, and it was let to three tenants. John and Margaret Shea had land at the town of Kilgobbin and along where the Ballyogan Road now runs, amounting to 115 statute acres. John O'Rourke held 255 statute acres at Kilgobbin and Jamestown, while Elizabeth Smith occupied 215 statute acres at Jamestown. Not content with splitting the Hutchinson holding seven ways, the seven parties split each of the three farms seven ways, creating a total of twenty one landholdings and massively increasing the cost and paperwork involved in renewing the lease on any of the three farms.

Two of the seven portions of land gradually became dispersed amongst several people and also dispersed geographically. By contrast, the other five portions converged on a single owner as the five sisters produced only two children between them, and these two married each other. However, tragically, it was not Henry O'Neill, the only child of the third generation, that came to own so much of the property, but his father, John Dawson O'Neill as Henry had died when only in his twenties.

John Dawson O'Neill was a borrower. Over a period he built up a substantial number of debts and was baled out financially on more than one occasion. It was sufficiently serious that the Rector of Kiltiernan stepped in and managed to get the family property held in trust to prevent it from being mortgaged any further. The O'Neills were the only descendants of the Dawson and Hutchinson families to have lived locally, but by 1840 they had moved out to live at various addresses in and around the city

Thomas Callaghan

Thomas Callaghan was a gentleman farmer. Born in about 1708, he farmed land at Ballyogan until 1747 when he increased his holding substantially with the addition of lands at Kilgobbin, leased from John Dawson. This new lease included 46 plantation acres known as Morris's farm and a further 6 acres once held by Richard Holland. In all, this made 52 plantation acres, equivalent to some 84 statute acres or about 34 hectares. Morris's farm was the land more recently occupied by the houses Greenfield, Elmfield and Larkfield, lying between Ballyogan Road and the river, and also included a section of the Gallops where the shopping centre and adjoining houses now stand. Holland's land was on the far side of Kilgobbin Road, including the future site of Kilgobbin House and the land behind it stretching alongside the river, where part of Sandyford Hall is now built.

Thomas Callaghan was obviously careful with his money as in 1762 he was in a position to lend £70 to his neighbour, Edward Webb, a sum equivalent to an entire year's rent on his Kilgobbin lands. To be on the safe side, the loan was registered as a mortgage on Edward Webb's land.

It is difficult for the modern observer to assess what happened next, for Thomas Callaghan became the victim of the instruments of oppression known collectively as the penal laws. After the Reformation in the mid 16th century various attempts had been made to stamp out Catholicism and non-conformist sects in these islands, though the severity of these laws varied from time to time, as did the degree of enforcement. The early to mid eighteenth century was a period when these laws were particularly strong, and amongst them were strict controls on Catholic rights to hold land. There was a maximum duration for which a lease which could be held by a Catholic and to help in enforcing this there was a facility known as *discovery*. This allowed a Protestant to apply to the courts to have himself declared the discoverer of the illegal holding of land by a Catholic. If the case was successfully proved, the court could confiscate the land holding and award it to the discoverer.

In Thomas Callaghan's case, the discoverer was Thomas Fleetwood from Kilbeggan in Westmeath, who filed his bill in the High Court of Chancery in September 1764 through an agent, Newton Bradford. Not content with Callaghan's own lands, Fleetwood's discovery also included Edward Webb's land as, even though Webb was not a Catholic, the registration of a mortgage on his land was technically equivalent to a lease for whatever duration the mortgagor held, which, in this case, was more than the legal maximum for a Catholic leaseholder. Having gained possession of a substantial tract of land in Kilgobbin, Fleetwood disposed of it to a painter from Dublin named John Briscoe.

That an act such as this could succeed is extraordinary when seen in context. Catholicism was practised legally and openly at this time and quite a number of Catholic chapels are marked on John Rocque's maps of this period. A few Catholic chapels existed in this general area such as at Old Connaught and at Cabinteely, not to mention closer to Kilgobbin at Newtown and Sandyford, as we have already noted. Catholic priests were respected members of society and their deaths were noted in the columns of the Dublin papers along with those of the gentry and the Anglican clergy. However, the relaxation of the penal laws may have started amongst the populace in general, but the statutes had not yet been amended. From 1772, some rights of landholding were granted to Catholics and in 1778 this was extended to allow the holding of leases of up to 999 years duration. Most of the penal laws had gone by 1793, but the last of them was not removed until 1829. In the 1760's, therefore, people like Thomas Fleetwood could make use of the laws for their own gain. Happily enough, while history does not relate exactly how it happened or when, both Thomas Callaghan and Edward Webb were in possession of their lands again before long.

Thomas Callaghan had one son, Robert, who also became a farmer. Robert Callaghan married in 1776 when he was 39 years of age and took over the farm. By this time Thomas Callaghan was 68 years old and was content to retire. He handed over his land, which by now included property at Murphystown and Carrickmines as well as Kilgobbin, and with it he gave Robert his cattle, cows, horses, cars, ploughs and utensils. To keep himself during his retirement he retained one cow and one horse with the liberty of grazing them, together with his own household goods, linen and clothes and a plot of land at Carrickmines on which to build himself a house, with an income of £30 a year from the lands. He may not have built this house at Carrickmines, as in March 1778 he took a lease on a house in the town of Kilgobbin, together with some small houses which would have been let to tenants to defray the rent on the property.

His retirement was shattered three years later when his son died at the age of 42. Thomas Callaghan returned to the life of running a large farm, but died not long afterwards in 1780, at the age of 72. It is uncertain whether Robert Callaghan produced children in his three years of marriage, but this is probable, as three Callaghan brothers held land in Ballyogan and Carrickmines in the early years of the following century, and it is possible that they were sons of Robert Callaghan's. They did not hold the Kilgobbin part of Thomas Callaghan's property, though, and this land came into the hands of a family named Shea.

The Shea family

It is not clear whether the Shea family was related to Thomas Callaghan. The family grave at Kilgobbin is the same one in which Robert Callaghan was buried and as Margaret Shea was just a year younger than him she could have been Robert Callaghan's sister, and Thomas Callaghan's daughter. There was some kind of connection in that the Sheas did not appear out of the blue. John Shea was a dairyman in the city, as was his father before him. They held 8 acres in what is now Upper Leeson Street and probably grazed their cows there. In 1777 John Shea assigned his land in Leeson Street to Thomas Callaghan, but why he did so is not clear.

The Sheas were certainly living at Kilgobbin before taking a formal lease on the lands once held by the Callaghans and Margaret Shea may have inherited the property following Thomas Callaghan's death. The lease was dated 13 October 1790 and was probably entered into in order to give them some security at a time of financial difficulties. In 1788 the entire family had mortgaged personal effects and two days after signing the lease on the former Callaghan lands they mortgaged the stock of corn and hay on the land for a massive £450. They subsequently took out further mortgages and it is possible that these moneys were being used to improve the property.

The Shea property was inherited by the surviving children, William and Alice, following the death of their mother in 1822. William Shea did not become a farmer like his parents. He married and left Kilgobbin to live in the city, taking a house at Montpelier Hill, near Parkgate Street. For a number of years he and his sister Alice let various parts of their lands at Kilgobbin to tenants. Part of their property had been leased early on in their time at Kilgobbin, including the land where Kilgobbin House and Kilgobbin Villa stand. With the cessation of the Shea family's farming activities, however, the balance was let out as land for the building of villas rather than farms, and three plots emerged, occupied by Greenfield, Elmfield and Larkfield.

Alice Shea never married and her share of the property eventually merged with her brother's. William Shea had nine children, three sons and six daughters. Following his death they inherited the property jointly and as two of them were living in Canada, one in the United States and others in various parts of Ireland they nominated one of the sons in law, Anthony Sutton, as trustee for their interests to make leases on their behalf and administer their property. The estate remained the property of William Shea's descendants until well into the twentieth century.

The Richardson family

The Richardsons were in Kilgobbin before the family became farmers. John

Richardson was a mason and a builder and built a number of houses locally including Larkfield and the original Elmfield. In the 1820's he was a churchwarden of Kilgobbin Church at the time when the new church at Kilternan was built and he was the contractor responsible for building that church. At that time he held not much more than one acre at Kilgobbin, and later in the 1820's he increased this with the addition of a further two acres adjoining the town. He also held almost three acres elsewhere.

Over time, the family increased its land holding substantially and collectively held one of the largest farms in the area. The largest single acquisition was of some 87 Irish acres to the north and west of Kilgobbin town which was leased from the Verner family, and this was followed by the taking of a lease of land to the south of Kilgobbin, now known as Clay Farm, in 1856. These two plots extend to a total of nearly 170 statute acres. The family is still prominent in the area.

The Doyle family and Murphystown

For some reason best known to history, leases of Murphystown were granted early in the eighteenth century to two people, each of whom held a half share in the land. Jeffrey Davis, a farmer based a Murphystown, acquired one share, and Morgan Maguire of Kilgobbin, also a farmer, got the other. It may be that there was a relationship between the two and that they inherited an earlier lease between them. The Davis family kept an interest in Murphystown for more than two centuries, and in the early twentieth century the family representative was Captain William Davis.

Morgan Maguire's family held its share until the late eighteenth century, but only just. In 1760 the property was in the hands of his widowed daughter-in-law, Elizabeth Maguire, who was a Catholic and fell prey to the system of "discovery" under the penal laws that we have already met. She lost her land to a "Protestant Discoverer", Edward Cullen, but the loss was not permanent. When Elizabeth Maguire died in the 1790's she bequeathed her share in Murphystown to various members of the Doyle family who were probably related, possibly being her grandchildren. John and James Doyle both lived at Barnacullia, their brother Joseph was a glazier in Dublin and their sister Sarah was married to a Dublin stonecutter named John Trumble. Another sister, Elizabeth had married John Booth, a Dublin merchant and both had died leaving two daughters and a son.

Over the years the Doyle family share in Murphystown became subdivided again and again. While there were always Doyles amongst the many owners of part shares, the marriage of a daughter of the family also brought in the families of Booth, Trumble, Walsh, Taylor, Curtis, Melvin, Somerville, Pike, Stewart, Mason, Ebbitt, Fitzsimons, Ryan, Tysdall and McEnnery. Many of these people were living in Barnacullia, Woodside or Murphystown, but there were several living in Dublin and another group in Longford. This kind of dispersal of the shares in the land left individuals holding one sixth of five twenty-fourths of a half share in Murphystown!

Matters were simplified in the early 1860's when an outsider named Frederick Stokes began to buy out the various shares. Bit by bit he re-assembled the landholding and having done so he sold the property to Joseph Wilson of Kilmacud who remained as ground landlord for many years. The Doyle family involvement in Murphystown ceased in 1862, but continued in Barnacullia, Woodside and elsewhere.

Landlords and tenants: an appraisal
By the 1850's the landlord system was on the way to being dismantled. The above summaries of some of the families illustrates the complexities that resulted from the system of land tenure. Taking the Fitzgerald landholding at Washington Lodge as an example at random the following diagrams illustrate the hierarchies of land ownership in the years 1700 and 1855:

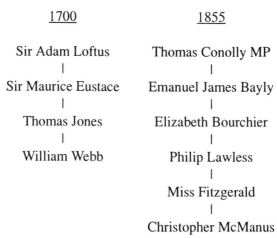

Fitzgerald property : Chain of land tenure

1700	1855
Sir Adam Loftus	Thomas Conolly MP
│	│
Sir Maurice Eustace	Emanuel James Bayly
│	│
Thomas Jones	Elizabeth Bourchier
│	│
William Webb	Philip Lawless
	│
	Miss Fitzgerald
	│
	Christopher McManus

Figure 8: *Hierarchy of tenancies on Fitzgerald property*

In 1700 William Webb was farming 121 plantation acres, subject to leases which went back through three landlords, each of whom was getting a cut of the rental. Already this seems to have involved unnecessary middlemen. By 1855, however, there were seven links in the chain. Christopher McManus, a stone cutter from Stepaside, was farming the land, paying his rent of £116 and 5 shillings a year to the two surviving daughters of David Fitzgerald. They paid a lesser sum to Philip Lawless, and so on up the line.

This system kept the gentry of the time as the leisured classes, particularly unmarried daughters, widows and retired professional men. It was a system that survives in a very much watered down form up to the present day and what the extensive reforms of the land law failed to change has been rendered of little import by the massive inflation of recent decades, as one of the major effects of the legal changes was to fix rents in perpetuity for many of the landlords. Examination of the census returns of the early years of this century reveals a substantial number of people who list their occupation as "income from property" or suchlike, though, even then, the rights of purchase given to tenants under the land acts had greatly reduced this category of incomes.

The above summary makes no attempt to analyse other aspects of the landlord system such as the rights of landlords to evict tenants and the lack of any rights for tenants to be compensated for improvements which they made to the land. These were other aspects which were tackled in the land acts of the later 19th century but no evidence seems to survive to suggest that they posed a particular problem in this area any more than they did elsewhere. For this we should be thankful!

10. THE EIGHTEENTH AND NINETEENTH CENTURIES

After the disruption of the wars of the 1640's, Ireland started on its move towards the modern age. The new king, Charles II, appointed the Duke of Ormonde as Lord Lieutenant for a second term in 1662 and the Duke started to develop Dublin into a modern city. Parliament began to meet more regularly and had a permanent base in Dublin, rather than meeting in various parts of the country such as Drogheda or Kilkenny. Dublin began to expand significantly outside its medieval walls and grew into a capital city with significant cultural events and a blossoming social elite.

As comparative peace and stability reigned, prosperity came with it. Improvements in technology brought greater mobility through improvements in the roads and in better means of transport and increased wealth allowed more people to travel. This did not happen overnight, and it was to be many years before it had a significant effect on the area that we are examining. The first areas to benefit from the changes were those that were suitable for industrial development. While there were windmills here and there, such as at Rathgar and Donnybrook, the main industrial centres were on rivers so as to avail of the water power they could provide. Many of these were on the Dodder and its larger tributaries, such as at Milltown, Clonskeagh, Rathfarnham and elsewhere. The river running off the mountain at Barnacullia into Kilgobbin and Jamestown would not have been large enough to support a mill of significant size. It is quite possible that Kilgobbin had a mill in medieval times, as a small scale mill grinding modest amounts of corn could be operated on this river near to Kilgobbin Castle and many of the castles would have had such a facility. However, the supply of water in the river would not have been sufficiently constant to allow for a mill which would compete on the open market as the mill would be restricted in the number of days a year it could operate and the flow of water would never allow it to grow into a large concern. The nearest mills to Kilgobbin in the eighteenth century were at Dundrum, Kilternan and Stillorgan, and there had previously been one at Carrickmines.

Another aspect of the growth in affluence was the building of large houses for the gentry outside the city. Many members of the gentry and aristocracy had their principal country seats in whatever part of Ireland the family estate happened to be and also kept a town house in Dublin. This led to a large increase in houses of the gentry in the city as the eighteenth century progressed and these are the famous Georgian houses of Dublin. As affluence continued to increase many of these people also provided themselves with a large country house close to the city so that they could retire out of Dublin at weekends, and even over night, while being within easy reach of the city to return to business when necessary. As is to be expected this tended to follow fashion and in the early eighteenth century the area around Blackrock was fashionable for its sea bathing. Increasingly, the area around Bray became popular, particularly later in the eighteenth century as regular scheduled coaches were introduced on that route. Other places also received their share of mansion houses and these became dotted around Stillorgan, Dundrum, Rathfarnham and so forth.

Our area did not benefit significantly from this trend. Until the late eighteenth century there were no houses of the gentry around Sandyford, Murphystown or Kilgobbin and the economy of the area was firmly based on farming, with stone cutting being the principal occupation towards the west on the slopes of Three Rock mountain. In this way, Kilgobbin, in particular, retained something of the flavour of the medieval settlement that it had been in the seventeenth century and before.

Various stories survive relating to Kilgobbin in the mid eighteenth century which illustrate its rural and agricultural nature. The historian Francis Elrington Ball related that Robert Jocelyn of Mount Merrion, future Earl of Roden, was part owner of a pack of hounds which were kennelled at Kilgobbin. The story has it that the pack was "overwhelmed by a mountain torrent" as described in a ballad dated 1st January 1748 entitled *An Elegy on a Pack of Hounds, whose kennel was situated at the foot of Kilgobbin....* Later writers have put the kennel in Kilgobbin Castle, but this is most unlikely as it is difficult to imagine how the castle could be overwhelmed by a mountain torrent, being on gently sloping ground more than a hundred metres from the small local river at a point where the river would need to flood to 180 metres in width to reach the castle.

Three years later a more drastic event occurred at Kilgobbin, though it may not have seemed so important in the minds of the young aristocracy as the loss of their beloved pack of hounds! In January 1751, according to a contemporary appeal, "a Fire broke in the house of Laurence Welsh, near Kilgobbin in the County of Dublin which reduced to ashes his dwelling house, cow house with 15 springing cows, as also a Barn and a Stable wherein were all his ploughs, cars and several other things convenient for a farmer and dairyman. A servant belonging to him was greatly singed by endeavering (sic) to quench the Fire, and said Welsh himself has one of his arms miserably burnt, and his knee out of Joint, and also several other Hurts, which he received, so that he and his servants lives are dispaired of - would it not be the greatest charity to assist the poor industrious man in his Time of great Distress?"

The Town of Kilgobbin

It seems remarkable that there was a town at Kilgobbin. Precisely what form this town took and what size it was is difficult to ascertain, but it was certainly not a large town and we might even refer to it as a small village. However, in Irish terminology the word town is used in relation to a settlement that might not even be classified as a village in another country. Later on, for example, in the nineteenth century, the Census returns classified a settlement as a town if it had at least twenty houses.

Officially, the use of the word *town* implies some form of administrative organisation such as a Corporation, or evidence of corporate action such as the erection of a town wall. There is no evidence that Kilgobbin fell into this category. Nevertheless, Kilgobbin was sufficiently important early in the eighteenth century to be considered to be a town and the word recurs in deeds of the area throughout that century. It is the norm in deeds to refer to townlands as "the town and lands of ...." although, frequently, there may be hardly a house in the townland and sometimes it might seem as if there had not been a house since Neolithic times! This phrase appears in relation to Kilgobbin, but there is a distinct difference in documents between "the town and lands of Kilgobbin" and "the town of Kilgobbin" and there is no ambiguity involved:- what is referred to is quite definitely a town.

Given that Kilgobbin had no industry to boost its economy or population, nor had it any country mansions, this town must have owed its existence to its farming hinterland, except for any income which could be gleaned from passing trade, for instance by an inn. As the town becomes increasingly less tangible in the records as the eighteenth century progresses, it would seem that it was in decline and it would seem reasonable to assume that its decline mirrored that of the castle. It also seems reasonable to take it one stage further and place the origins of the town at the time when the castle was in its prime at some time between the fifteenth and seventeenth centuries. It was in the seventeenth century that many of the medieval settlements fell into decline and often they disappeared altogether. This seems to have been the pattern at Kilgobbin, with decline rather than abandonment occurring. Its existence at the end of the medieval period is implied in a map included in *Pacata Hibernia*, published in 1633, in which "Kilgoban" is one of only four places marked in the whole of the south County Dublin. The suggestion is that Kilgobbin was one of the more significant places in the south county and this, in turn, implies a town of some kind.

The first specific mention of the town of Kilgobbin in registered deeds relating to the area was in 1730, when the land leased to John Dawson by executors of Richard Nutley included seven acres of land "lying about the town of Kilgobbin". That there was no earlier deed registered that referred to the town is not surprising as very few deeds relating to the general area had been registered since the establishment of the Registry of Deeds in 1708 and this was the first time that land in the town had been the subject of a registered deed.

Over time a number of mentions are made of the town, many of them being repeats of the same seven acre plot, but others also appear. The seven acre plot includes "cabbins and gardens ...... together with the old castle". In 1747 there is a reference to a meadow which "adjoins the great road in the street of Kilgobbin" and this also refers to "part of the Green". Later on there is a mention of "the old Pound of Kilgobbin", and this would have been where animals were impounded either when they were stray or when they were confiscated because of debts that were unpaid. There was also an inn from at least the early eighteenth century and this was possibly in existence by the end of the seventeenth century. The details of this inn will be discussed later.

So, from the evidence of deeds, we can piece together something of the town of Kilgobbin. It had a castle, an inn, a village green, a pound and several houses or cabins, but how many of these is impossible to determine as the smaller houses always appear lumped together in documents as "several cabins" or "all those cabins belonging to....". There was also the church, of course, but the town was adjacent to the castle and the church was at some distance from them. Shops as we know them would not have existed in the seventeenth and early eighteenth centuries and such retail establishments as there were would not have appeared in official records.

Where was the town? It is difficult to be specific about its exact location or size at most periods of its existence, but it lay approximately between the castle and Oldtown House. It seems to have been predominantly situated along the road rather than back towards the castle, at least in the mid eighteenth century as can be seen on John Rocque's map of 1760 (Figure 9, page 73). This map shows four buildings alongside the road, three on the north side with the castle visible to the rear, and a fourth, L-shaped building on the south side. This latter building was the inn and seems to have a garden to its western side, a feature which may still be seen today. The earlier deeds relating to the inn put it on the same side of the road as the castle. This is not to suggest that the inn was replaced by a new building on the other side of the road, but that the road itself moved. The road is stated to be the southern boundary of the property in those deeds, though later on, before Rocque's map, the road moved to sever the property. This helps to explain why Oldtown House has its entrance on the far side from the road. The absence of any buildings immediately next to the castle at that time is also seen quite clearly in Gabriel Beranger's watercolour of the castle taken in 1766 and, later, in George Petrie's engraving of 1819.

The Inn

Curiously, the word *inn* never appears throughout all of the registered deeds relating to Kilgobbin. The evidence for its existence comes from a little further afield. There was a farmer in Jamestown named Darby Moran who, in 1719, ran into financial difficulties. His brother, George Moran, went security for him "to several persons for several considerable sums of money" and, in return, Darby Moran assigned his farm at Jamestown to his brother. George Moran later mortgaged the property and after his death his widow disposed of the property to John Dawson. Where this is relevant is that in the transactions relating to Kathleen Moran's disposal of the property she is referred to as the widow of George Moran of Kilgobbin, innkeeper.

Once we know that the innkeeper was George Moran we can identify the inn. At the end of the seventeenth century Edward Moran took a lease from Thomas Jones of about 7 acres of land at the town of Kilgobbin. This land included the castle and seems also to have included most, if not all, of the town. The inn seems to have been built at around that time. A few years ago

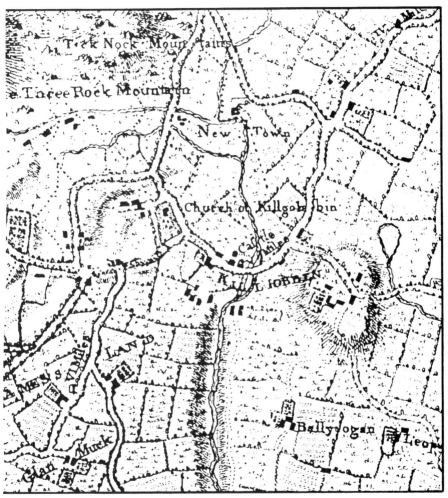

Figure 9. John Rocque's map (1760)

during alterations to the house workmen discovered a coin dated 1693 in the roof. Assuming that this was lost there during the building of the house and that it was of comparatively recent date at the time it suggests that the house was built in the 1690's, perhaps when Edward Moran took the lease.

Between Edward and George Moran they held the property for thirty years until George Moran's death in the late 1720's. The inn then passed through a number of hands in the mid eighteenth century. By the middle of the century it is clear that the inn was known as *The White House* or *The White House of Kilgobbin*, and it may well be that this name dates from the time that it was owned by the Morans.

Oldtown House, former White House Inn

Kilgobbin lay on the road to Enniskerry and Powerscourt. In the eighteenth century, just as now, Powerscourt had fine gardens which were open to public view, as was the waterfall, which was a popular tourist spot. Parties of visitors would make the journey out from the city to Enniskerry and they were in need of refreshment and a change of horses along the way. Villages such as Milltown benefited from this passing trade and so did Kilgobbin. Travel at the time included a system known as the *Post Chaise*, a *Post* being a stopping point. If one travelled by post chaise this would involve stopping at intervals to change over to a fresh team of horses for the carriage. Along post chaise routes there were inns at which this procedure was carried out and the White House at Kilgobbin was one. The fare for travelling by post chaise was based on the distance travelled and milestones were erected to mark the intervals along the route. There is still a milestone at Kilgobbin, on the bend in the road alongside Kilgobbin House, to remind us of this former practice. The stone bears no inscription other than the number "5", which is the distance from the city in Irish miles. The Irish mile was approximately two kilometres, or one and a quarter statute miles, and was in use, like the Irish acre, until the middle nineteenth century. The Irish mile is still sometimes referred to by older people.

It is unclear when the inn ceased to be used as such. Mrs Rose Field took a lease on it in 1792 and held it until her death in 1822 and she may have been the last innkeeper. However, it is also possible that she occupied it as a private house. At the time of her death the viability of an inn at this location would have been threatened by the imminent construction of the Enniskerry Road connecting Sandyford directly with Stepaside and bypassing Kilgobbin and it would seem logical that this would be when the inn closed.

The demise of Kilgobbin town

As we have seen, Kilgobbin town seems to have been declining through the eighteenth century. Even up to the beginning of the nineteenth century the town retained some semblance of its status. Archer's *Statistical Survey of the County Dublin*, published in 1800, includes a map of the county on which various places are marked. Kilgobbin is about the only place marked on the map within the south east of the county other than those on the coast or the Dodder and places such as Dundrum are noticeably absent. It should be added, though, that Archer described Kilgobbin as "a small village".

In common with the inn, Kilgobbin seems to have been eclipsed by Stepaside as a result of the new Enniskerry Road in the 1820's. Both Stepaside and Sandyford were in existence long before the coming of the road and Sandyford was also bypassed, though not as severely as Kilgobbin. Having lost its inn in favour of Stepaside, Kilgobbin began to lose out in other ways. When the Irish Constabulary was set up in the 1830's it was

Stepaside that got the new Police Barracks and with the barracks came the village pound, replacing Kilgobbin's. Kilgobbin had a shop until the 1840's, but it seems to have gone at that time. Stepaside had a forge, a shop and a shoemaker and gradually increased the number of businesses.

Kilgobbin did not die, however, but became a residential village. There had been cabins in the village since at least the seventeenth century, as we have seen, and these were replaced gradually with newer cottages. A number of houses also appeared, bringing a new life to the village and by about 1850 Kilgobbin had taken on the form that is recognisable today. Not everyone was pleased with this change. An amateur artist, Charles Pratt, sketched the castle at Kilgobbin in 1806 and in later years, when describing what he had sketched, he said that the foreground and middle distance were "now either shut out or disfigured by building plantations and enclosures".

One main instigator of the changes in Kilgobbin town in the nineteenth century was Margaret Cuthbert. She moved to Kilgobbin in 1823 from Dublin, following the death of her husband, Richard Cuthbert. The land she acquired was part of the property of the Hutchinson family that had been allocated to Mathew Bellew under the agreement in 1797 to divide up the property. The land included portions on each side of the road, including the old inn on the south side and the castle on the north. She set about improving the property to provide herself with an income from rents. There was a lane known as *Castle Lane* leading from the road to the castle and Mrs Cuthbert erected a line of cottages along this lane. Alongside the lane and to the east she built two more substantial houses which were let to various tenants over the years. Finally, in 1831, she leased the balance of the land to Emanuel Bayly who built a fine villa with the remains of the old castle in the grounds.

The Cuthbert family remained in Kilgobbin for a number of years. Mrs Cuthbert had three daughters and a son who lived on in Kilgobbin after her death. The son, Rev. George G Cuthbert, is frequently quoted in writings about the area as he wrote reminiscences of Kilgobbin. It was his sisters, Frances, Jesse and Cecilia, however, who controlled the family property. They had moved to Kilgobbin as young children and stayed for the rest of their lives. Frances died in 1864, Jesse in 1875 and Cecilia in 1880. The property was inherited by two friends of Cecilia's who lived in England and who sold off the premises in separate lots.

Other buildings in Kilgobbin

Apart from the castle and the church, which were now ruined, and the inn, which had been converted to a private house, Kilgobbin had few non-residential buildings in the nineteenth century. As we have noted, most of these tended to be located on the route to Enniskerry at Stepaside, rather than in the now-bypassed Kilgobbin.

The schools which were provided did not come to Kilgobbin town. The Church of Ireland parish school was built in 1818-9 as one of the improvements brought about by Rev Henry Kearney following his arrival in the parish in 1817. At that time it was common for schools and charities to get at least part of their funding from charity sermons. These were sermons delivered, usually by an invited guest speaker and usually on an annual basis, for the purpose of raising money through a collection from the congregation. Donations at these affairs were usually generous and the event could provide a substantial amount of the running cost of a school. Another means of funding came from charitable organisations which were set up for the purpose and which were frequently veiled forms of proselytising. Whatever their shortcomings they did provide much-needed income for schools at a time when the general standard of literacy was low and most people could not afford to pay for schooling.

The parish school at Kilgobbin was built on a site opposite the church and provided education for boys and girls separately, as was the norm at the time. Part of the cost of building it came from charity sermons in the various parts of the district that sent children to the school. The income for running it came from one of the charitable organisations called *The Association for Discountenancing Vice* and from the Lord Lieutenant's Fund and these would have provided the £10 a year which the teachers were paid in the early years. The master and mistress lived in an adjoining house with a garden which the master reclaimed from an old gravel pit at his own expense. They taught an average of twenty children each and these children contributed a penny a week towards their schooling, if they could afford it. It is interesting that although this was a Church of Ireland school, the Ordnance Survey in the 1830's reported that most of the pupils were Catholic.

In 1821, two years after the establishment of Kilgobbin school, the census listed some 108 pupils at schools in the parish, 66 males and 42 females. These cannot all have been at Kilgobbin parish school, and it is likely that the Catholic church was also running its own school. At that time there were frequently schools run by private individuals, not just for the private education of the children of the gentry, but also for the education of ordinary people. There may have been some of these in the parish.

A school for the Catholic parish of Sandyford and Glencullen was erected at Sandyford in 1840 as a result of a legacy from Lord Castlecoote who had lived at Leopardstown Park. He bequeathed £500 for the building of the school and a further £500 as a capital sum to provide an income for its running costs. As with the Kilgobbin school, the boys and girls were taught separately at Sandyford. This school was replaced by a new school building in 1936. The teacher's house, now a pre-school, was built in 1889.

There was also a dispensary, located initially at Stepaside. The dispensaries that appeared in the early to mid nineteenth century provided the main form of health care for most of the populace. They were initially supported partly by public subscription and partly by the grand jury, which was the precursor of the local authority. In the *laissez faire* times of the nineteenth century public funds for facilities such as health and education were limited and, as we have seen, charity was a major factor in providing these services. Later on, responsibility was taken for them by the Poor Law Unions, which, in our case, meant the Rathdown Union. The medical attendants at the dispensary lived locally in Kilgobbin and later in the nineteenth century a new dispensary and medical attendant's residence were built at Violet Hill, near Kilgobbin.

Roads

We tend to take our roads for granted and rarely question when they were built or by whom. Unless we can remember a road being built we tend to assume that it has always been there. However, roads have changed considerably over the years and some roads are considerably older than others. In the past roads could be classified into local access roads and those which led further afield, just as they can now. The main road from Dublin to Enniskerry led through the area, as we have already seen. It passed through Dundrum and Sandyford before reaching Kilgobbin and continuing via Stepaside towards Enniskerry along its present line, except that it did not pass through the Scalp until the late eighteenth century due to the engineering problems of building a road through the Scalp. Instead, the road went over the hillside to the east. Ballinteer Road is also of some antiquity, as is Stepaside Hill, which formed the main access to Glencullen.

At the end of the eighteenth and beginning of the nineteenth century there was a boom in new road building. This was partly for military reasons as the government sought to improve the mobility of troops in the 1790's in case of an invasion by the French. A large military camp was established at Loughlinstown at that time to enable swift response to an invasion. A few years later the Martello towers along the coast were built as a new defence system against invasion and troop movements still needed to be flexible. To add to this the 1798 rebellion added internal strife as a reason for needing speedy military response and the military road to Wicklow through Glencree was built at this time. A second reason for needing new roads was the improvements in transport. Mail coaches had been introduced in the 1780's on many trunk routes, leading to widening and straightening existing roads and the building of new roads or new bypasses. Even where there was no mail coach or stage coach routes private coach transport was increasing and this led to pressure for new roads. Private transport also included the movement of goods and this included, in the case of the Barnacullia area, an increasing amount of building stone being transported to the building sites, mostly in the city.

There were several new roads in the area at this time. These included Ballyogan Road and Glenamuck Road. A little later, in the 1820's, Enniskerry Road was built as a wider, less twisty, bypass of the Kilgobbin Road. While the new road climbed higher than the old one the gradient was better as it avoided Sandyford Hill and it was therefore more readily used for horse-drawn vehicles.

Blackglen Road and Hillcrest Road are 19th century roads, built to replace the earlier route which ran from Sandyford cross-roads a little to the south of Hillcrest Road and joined up with Slate Cabin Lane to lead up the hillside towards Ticknock. At this time, as now, the road from Stillorgan to Kilgobbin was along Brewery Road and Murphystown Road, but the only part of Leopardstown Road that existed was along the section between those two roads. It was only in the second quarter of the nineteenth century that the section of Leopardstown Road leading to Sandyford Cross was built and the final section connecting to Whites Cross was later again.

Locally, around Kilgobbin, the local access roads have also changed. Kilgobbin Lane leading from the town of Kilgobbin past the old church led, in the eighteenth century, on up the hillside to Barnacullia. This route survives as a pedestrian right of way, but only because of the efforts of local people to keep it open. In 1861 the occupier of Fern Hill, Alderman Darley, sought to close off the access in order to enlarge his gardens and it was only after the matter came to court that the pathway was kept open. Later attempts by the Alderman's son, Judge Darley and his grandson, Edmund S Darley, to divert and close off the access also led to a lawsuit. As a result, the lane is sunken through much of the Fern Hill estate to keep it separate from the demesne, and passes under a tunnel in one place where an avenue at Fern Hill crosses the lane.

Leading off the lane Burrow Road now leads up to Ballyedmonduff, but it is also a road that dates from the nineteenth century, being provided at the same time as Enniskerry Road and giving a more direct route to Glencullen, though bypassing Stepaside.

An earlier road that has now disappeared led from Stepaside to the old village of Kilternan. This village was near the early church which is now in ruins alongside Bishop's Lane, off Glencullen Road. What we now know as Bishop's Lane is a cul-de-sac, leading not far beyond the old church. However, this led on to Stepaside along a route mid way between Enniskerry Road and Ballyedmonduff Road. Ballyedmonduff Road itself is a replacement for an earlier route and was constructed in the 1830's. At that time the Ordnance Survey described the old route as a rough rocky road and commented that "a new road is about to be made to which the inhabitants seem very unwilling".

Another local road that no longer exists was a laneway around the hillock on which the old church of Kilgobbin stands. This lane was there in the mid eighteenth century and left the church on an island site surrounded by roads and survives in part as the field access alongside the cross. There was also a road leading from Enniskerry Road to Glenamuck and Carrickmines through Jamestown. This would have led off Enniskerry Road near Stepaside Golf Course and probably disappeared towards the end of the eighteenth century when the Rorke family developed the lands around their new mansion at Jamestown House.

Stepaside

The village of Stepaside grew up in the mid eighteenth century. It is normal for various services to locate at cross roads, or at least at a T-junction, in order to get the maximum benefit from passing trade, and the junction of Kilgobbin Road with Stepaside Hill would have been no exception.

The Step Inn, Stepaside

John Rocque's map of 1760 shows two or three buildings where Kilgobbin Road and Stepaside Hill meet. It is not possible to tell from the map whether these were single buildings or, perhaps pairs of semi-detached or terraced houses. Groups of buildings such as these are common on any map, including Rocque's, and does not necessarily imply a village. At what stage the group of buildings came to be considered as a place that should have a name is uncertain, but the earliest record of the name *Stepaside* that seems to survive is in the 1780's. A deed dated 1785 mentions Stepaside in a list of lands being mortgaged, though the same family's deed of acquisition of the property in 1749 had listed the lands without the name Stepaside. At around the same time people started giving Stepaside as their address. In the 1790's an inn was established and was named *The Kilgobbin Inn*. This is now known to us as *The Step Inn*.

In the nineteenth century Stepaside was certainly a significant village. Taylor's map of the environs of Dublin, dated 1816, not only shows the buildings but labels the village "Stepaside" (Figure 10). By about this time the village had fourteen houses and it continued to grow. In the 1830's the Ordnance Survey reported that Stepaside had "three miserable public houses, a Police Barrack and a Smith's forge with about half a dozen cabins". There were twenty six houses by 1841. In 1848 there were twenty seven houses, one of which was in ruins and there was also the Police Barracks, a pound and two shops. The numbers of houses fell before picking up again to peak at 33 houses in 1861, following which the number gradually fell again to the end of the century. The number of people living in Stepaside also followed this pattern, reaching a peak of almost two hundred people in 1861 and tailing off to only 87 in 1901.

What happened to bring about the dramatic fall in the number of houses in the late 1840's was not the catastrophic famine of the time, but comprehensive redevelopment, as we would now call it. John Clements lived in Stepaside at the southern end of the village, close to where the pedestrian crossing is now. He was a shoemaker and kept a provision shop and also had a line of houses along the eastern side of the road, between his house and the Step Inn. In the 1840's he built a range of new cabins on his property and it is unlikely that they were occupied by the time of the 1851 census. John Rooney owned the Step Inn where he also had a provision shop and, like John Clements, he built a range of new cabins in the 1840's. Across the road at the foot of Stepaside Hill, Nicholas McHugh had the village forge, close to the dispensary.

Also alongside Stepaside Hill was the constabulary barracks. The Irish Constabulary had been established in 1836 and was later to be known as the Royal Irish Constabulary. The barracks at Stepaside was established at the very beginning of the Constabulary's history and it came into the news in 1867 during the Fenian rising. A party of Fenians captured some constabulary men and marched on Stepaside barracks and laid siege to it. Eventually the constables in the barracks surrendered and were taken prisoner, following which the Fenian force marched on the RIC barracks at Glencullen to repeat their success. The old barracks building no longer exists and there is a modern house on the site. However, the walls of the pound are still there alongside the site of the barracks, just up the hill from the shop.

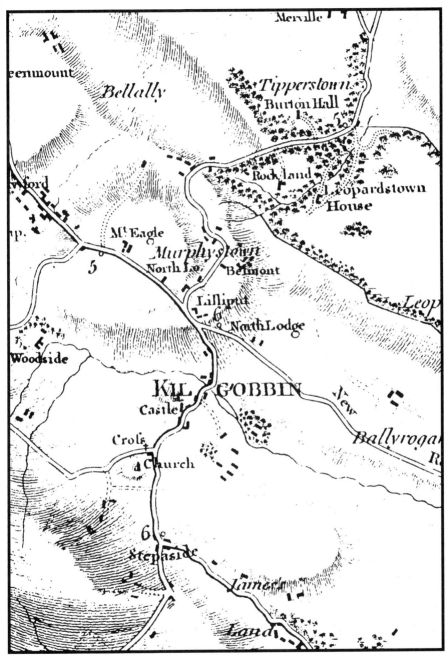

Figure 10. John Taylor's map of The Environs of Dublin (1816) [enlarged]

The old Animal pound at Stepaside

The inhabitants of Stepaside included those who were providing the services such as shops and crafts. Of the remainder, some were farm labourers, but also tenant farmers holding land in the vicinity. There was also quite a number of stone cutters, this being the principal occupation in the area after farming.

Population

The census which we know today was started in 1801 and has continued almost uninterrupted every ten years since then. The first attempts were of dubious accuracy, particularly in the more remote areas that were inhospitable to the government employees that sought the information. For our purposes we will start with the census of 1821, though details were only available on a parish basis in that census and in 1831. Information relating to individual townlands is available from 1841 onwards.

There were 165 houses in the parish of Kilgobbin in 1821, occupied by 176 families, with 1021 persons. The number of houses in the parish fluctuated somewhat during the century, reaching a maximum of 197 in 1871 and falling back to 166 by 1911. The population of the parish stayed extremely constant throughout the century, rising to a maximum of 1207 in 1861, but in any other census remaining between 1012 and 1077 - a remarkable consistency. After the end of the century it fell, though, to 928 in 1901 and 910 in 1911. The stability of the total population and the comparative stability in the number of houses is all the more remarkable when we look at the individual townlands as many of them were anything but stable. The stability of the overall total, then, is nothing but pure coincidence.

The first years for which townland populations are available were 1841 and 1851, allowing us to see the change during the famine years of the 1840's. Curiously, all of the townlands in Kilgobbin, with the exception of Barnacullia and Kilgobbin itself, actually *gained* population during the famine. This is at total variance with even the reasonably prosperous areas of south east Dublin, and becomes inexplicable when we look at a remote mountain area like Ballybrack which gained 10% population in that decade. Neighbouring mountain townlands such as Boranaraltry and Brockey also gained at that time, though the adjoining areas of Ballybetagh and Kilternan lost 33% and 22% respectively. Kilgobbin, with Stepaside, lost a staggering 40% of its population during the famine years, but soon picked up again. Excluding Stepaside, Kilgobbin townland continued to lose population, falling from 222 in 1841 to 101 in 1871 and gradually climbing back to 224 in the 1911 census. Barnacullia lost a quarter of its population in the 1840's but built back up by 1881, possibly due to the increased call for stone in building and paving. The extremes were Jamestown which increased its population from 5 to 65 in the ten years from 1841 to 1851, and Woodside which went from 13 to 107 in that decade before falling back to 32 in 1881.

The number of occupied houses increased and decreased with the population. Kilgobbin and Stepaside lost about half of their houses in the 1840's, from 72 in 1841 to 39 in 1851, bouncing back to 60 in 1861. This may be largely because of rebuilding, as many of Mrs Cuthbert's cottages were empty in the mid 1840's, and changed tenants in that time. On the other hand, it may reflect famine disaster amongst her tenants. At Stepaside there certainly was a significant amount of rebuilding in that decade as we have seen.

Figure 11: CENSUS: Kilgobbin Parish

Townland populations

	1821	1831	1841	1851	1861	1871	1881	1891	1901	1911
Ballybrack			205	226	249	205	184	161	120	108
Ballyedmonduff	199		251	244	220	170	162	179	164	
Barnacullia			204	155	235	285	347	319	289	291
Jamestown			5	65	63	50	23	28	33	40
Kilgobbin			222	222	131	101	110	154	144	224
Newtown Little		15	20	25	25	26	35	18	18	
Woodside			13	107	65	36	32	68	58	65
K'gn par.	**1021**	**1149**	**1012**	**1049**	**1207**	**1077**	**1063**	**1017**	**928**	**910**
Stepaside			149		195	155	171	90	87	-

Townland occupied houses

	1821	1831	1841	1851	1861	1871	1881	1891	1901	1911
Ballybrack			32	32	37	35	33	30	29	26
Ballyedmonduff		34	36	34	39	29	24	23	26	
Barnacullia			39	24	38	50	57	48	49	45
Jamestown			1	13	10	11	5	6	8	9
Kilgobbin			46	39	27	21	23	34	28	47
Newtown Little		2	5	4	5	5	5	5	3	
Woodside			-	17	9	8	9	11	10	10
K'gbbin par	**165**	**176**	**182**	**166**	**192**	**197**	**190**	**178**	**171**	**166**
Stepaside		14		26	<20	33	28	29	20	19

Sandyford

Sandyford seems to have its origins at least as far back as the seventeenth century. The name is also at least that old. The name "Sandyford" was already in existence by 1699 when it was part of lands included in a lease. Frequently a place name applies to quite a small area and has no significance in the hierarchy of administrative areas used for local government. Such was the case with Sandyford which not alone was not a townland in its own right, but straddled the townland boundaries to find itself divided between two civil parishes. To the south it consisted of 17 acres in the parish of Kilgobbin, while its northern portion was in Balally, in the parish of Taney. The village itself grew up predominantly in the Taney portion, though it later spread into the Kilgobbin portion and also into a third parish, as the east side of Sandyford Hill is in Blackthorn townland, Tully parish.

At this distance it is difficult to tell whether Sandyford village grew up around the Catholic Chapel, or whether the chapel was established in the village. We have seen how there was a history of Catholic worship in the district after the Reformation and how a chapel was established at Sandyford at least as early as 1731 during the height (or depth) of penal times. John Rocque's map of Dublin County of 1760 shows only a few buildings at Sandyford and they do not seem to form a village. It is probable, therefore, that the village grew up as a result of the existence of the chapel. By the time of John Taylor's map of 1816, Sandyford was shown as a village of respectable size and appeared to be larger than either Kilgobbin or Stepaside at that date.

Sandyford was not a major village and tended to be little more than a haphazard cluster of cottages. Neither the historian John D'Alton nor Samuel Lewis in his *Topographical Dictionary of Ireland* threw much light on the appearance of Sandyford village when they wrote in 1838 and 1837 respectively. However, the Ordnance Survey had visited in 1836 and reported that there was a provision store, two public houses and the chapel. The Ordnance Survey's reporter, Lieutenant Bennett, was unenthusiastic, though, and described it as "a poor village". No doubt Sandyford was still feeling the effects of being bypassed by the construction of the Enniskerry Road in the early 1820's, which favoured Stepaside rather than Sandyford with the passing trade.

Sandyford got its own post office in the 1880's under the sub-postmaster,

Thomas Burton. He was from Co. Wicklow originally and had lived for some time in Scotland where he married and where his daughter Alice Mary Burton was born. In 1895 he acquired about 6½ acres on Sandyford Hill and here he built a house and set up a new post office. After his death in about 1903 the post office was taken over by his daughter, Alice. She had trained as a telegraphist and had been working in the post office since she was in her teens. Around 1916 Alice married Frank Pigott, a cycle and motor engineer, who seems to have been a son or grandson of the infamous Richard Pigott who had shot himself in 1889 after confessing to having forged letters to *The Times* purporting to implicate Parnell in the Phoenix Park murders.

Barnacullia

The area around Barnacullia with its focus on the granite quarries has been described in Nicholas Ryan's recent book *Sparkling Granite*. Before the days of machines that could cut granite to fine detail, the cutting of this hard stone was extremely labour intensive and so it tended to be used for more straight forward work. While many of the principal public buildings in Dublin use granite, the more decorative portions of many of them, such as the Custom House and the Bank of Ireland, tend to use other materials such as the softer Portland Stone. The quarries at Barnacullia were renowned for their paving stone which was in great demand for footpaths in the city and the kerbstones that separated them from the carriageways. While the rectangular *setts* (frequently incorrectly referred to as cobbles) were a common feature of the city streets, these were not generally made of granite. Some are of granite, others were laid down with Bray Stone, which is a hard quartzite, but in the main they are of imported Welsh stone which was favoured by the paving board and the Corporation for its wearing qualities. Later in the nineteenth century, and, more particularly, in the twentieth, granite has become more widely used for decorative stonework, and some of this comes from the local quarries at Barnacullia.

A great deal of the land at Barnacullia was farmed and many a family of stonecutters also held farming land, though often this was only a small plot. In the middle of the nineteenth century the Ordnance Survey reported that in Barnacullia agriculture was "very little attended to". Barnacullia was said to have only one narrow lane leading along a line of granite quarries. The land was reported to be "set in lots of from five to fifty acres to rough stone cutters whose principal employment is to quarry out stones and cut them according to the orders they receive from the Dublin Paving Board, from (twenty to thirty shillings) a week can be earned but they generally only work the three latter days of the week". This last comment is not explained!

11. HOUSES

We have already seen how the improvements in means of transport led to an increase in the number of people not involved in agriculture who were living in country houses close to the city. Initially these were the very wealthy who could afford not only a second or third house, but also the means of transport to the city. As transport improved it became cheaper and it became possible for a wider range of people to live in houses in the country.

In this section we will look at some of the principal houses in our area. This does not aim to provide a detailed history of each of the houses, but to give some idea of when they were built and in what circumstances. They are included here in alphabetical order, and as we will see some of them were intended as farm houses while others were country villas of the gentry.

Bayly's Cabin

see *Kilgobbin Castle*

Belmont House

See *Clonlea*

Castle Lodge

This house was one of a pair, with Thornberry, built by Margaret Cuthbert following her acquisition of land at Kilgobbin in 1823. She also built a row of cottages alongside the house in the 1840's and the cottages went with the house in the Cuthberts' time and through the subsequent occupation. Castle Lodge was occupied by the Cuthberts themselves for a time, and was subsequently let to tenants. For a substantial period it was occupied by the successive local dispensary doctors. After the death of Cecilia Cuthbert Castle Lodge was sold to Patrick Corcoran and the cottages at Castle Lane became known as Corcoran's Cottages for a time.

Clay Farm

This house seems to have been built around 1820 by Eaton Cotter. He took leases on a number of plots of land in Kilgobbin in the early years of the nineteenth century as described above in discussing the Webb family. Following initial problems with gaining vacant possession of part of the land that was held by John Rorke, William Webb had handed over land to Eaton Cotter in 1809. In 1818, following John Rorke's bankruptcy William Webb had possession of the land and was able to make a new lease to Eaton Cotter which included a plot of land extending to 34 acres, in addition to other land. It would seem that Eaton Cotter built the house at this stage, as it does not appear on Taylor's map of *The Environs of Dublin* published in 1816.

In 1822 Eaton Cotter leased to John David Mowlds some 34 acres "with all houses buildings and improvements erected thereon". John D Mowlds had been living at Shankill, but his family came from Milltown where they had been since 1720 when John Moules, a dairyman from Donnybrook, acquired a farm there. John D Mowlds lived on the property for the more than twenty years, and at about the same time as he moved in his brother, George Frederick Mowlds came to live on the adjoining land of Larkfield.

In the mid 1830's, John D Mowlds ran into financial problems. He mortgaged the property to George Frederick Mowlds in March 1835 and George F Mowlds assigned his mortgage to their brother in law, John Hunt, a few months later. The loan was not sufficient to solve his problems in the longer term and in 1839 John D Mowlds was imprisoned in the Four Courts Marshalsea in Dublin for his debts. The Four Courts Marshalsea was a debtors prison located off Thomas Street near to the Guinness brewery and at that time one could be incarcerated at the behest of a creditor until the debts were paid. The creditor in this case was William Elliott Hudson, a barrister, of Fitzwilliam Street. He agreed to accept a mortgage on the property provided George F Mowlds and John Hunt assigned their interest in the property to him. In effect, William E Hudson became the John D Mowlds' landlord.

In 1844, John D Mowlds sold his remaining interest in the property to Frederick G Barton and moved back to Milltown. In 1856, following William E Hudson's death, his executors conveyed the property to John Richardson, whose descendants have occupied it to the present day. The house was comparatively modest at this time but was rebuilt in 1869 when it became known as *Clay Farm*.

Clonlea

Clonlea stands on Murphystown Road and originates from 1787 when a watchmaker named George Walker took a lease of two little fields at Murphystown. On them he built himself a house which he named Belmont House. The Walker family lived there for two generations before disposing of it in 1828. The house went through a number of ownerships over the years and also a few changes of name. In the mid nineteenth century it was known as Murphystown Lodge and it became known as Clonlea towards the end of the century. Clonlea was a more modest sized house initially and took on its present size and appearance in 1905.

Cottage Park

see *Lisieux*

Elmfield House

Elmfield, in common with Larkfield, was a product of the cessation of use of the Shea lands for farming in the 1820's. George Mahon occupied a house on the property for a time and a variety of occupiers followed. The house was modest to start with and was described by the Ordnance Survey in the 1830's as "a comfortable little house". It was enlarged in the 1860's by Henry Moss who had acquired the property in 1856. The house was demolished and rebuilt on a much larger scale in 1914.

Fern Hill

The original house at Fern Hill was built by the Alderman Frederick Darley. In 1815 he acquired the lease of the townland of Newtown Little which had previously been farmed. The house was not shown on John Taylor's map of the Environs of Dublin which was published in 1816 and it must have been built shortly after that date. The Darleys had a long history of involvement in the building industry, mainly as builders, but some of their number had also been architects. At Fern Hill they exploited the natural resources of their land by opening up granite quarries on the hill slopes above the house. They held their land as tenants of the Verner family and acted as land agents for the Verners who were based in county Armagh. The demesne of Fern Hill was laid out as fine gardens by the Darleys and on two occasions they achieved notoriety for attempts to block off the right of way through their property as we have seen already. After more than a hundred years in occupation the Darley property was sold to the Walker family in the 1930's and the tradition of finely landscaped gardens continues.

Glenbourne

After the death of Judge Murphy of Glencairn (see below) his widow leased some eight Irish acres along Ballyogan Road to Nathaniel Hone. By 1904, he had built Glenbourne for his own occupation. The amount of land that accompanied the house was radically reduced in 1907 when Nathaniel Hone sold more than six acres back to Richard Croker, the Murphys' successor at Glencairn, as part of his assembly of land to provide his Gallops.

Glencairn

In 1859 George Gresson took a lease of a large amount of land at Murphystown. He engaged one of the best architects of the day, Benjamin Woodward, to design a large, fine house. Woodward was in partnership with Thomas Deane, though Deane tended to be the businessman of the partnership while Woodward had the design flair as an architect. Having designed the new university buildings in Cork they moved to Dublin where their most famous works were the Museum Building in Trinity College and the Kildare Street Club. They designed a number of notable buildings before Benjamin Woodward's untimely death in 1860 at the age of only forty four. Some of these, such as the very fine Rathmichael Parish Church, were not started until after Woodward's death, but nonetheless display his qualities as an architect. George Gresson's house was under construction during Woodward's lifetime. Work probably started in 1859 and was certainly under way by early 1860.

George Gresson was a solicitor with a practice in Upper Merrion Street. He lived at Glencairn until his death in the mid 1870's. His successor in the house was a barrister, James Murphy, who bought the house in 1877 for £9,000. In 1879 he married Mary Keogh, daughter of the late Judge William

Keogh, formerly a judge in the Court of Common Pleas. Judge Keogh had been a Member of Parliament, a founder of the Catholic Defence Association and a supporter of tenant rights. He had held the offices of Solicitor General and Attorney General before being appointed to the bench. His most famous task in that office was to try the Fenian leaders in 1865. He committed suicide a few months before his daughter's marriage. James Murphy rose through the legal ranks to become a High Court Judge. After his death his widow lived on in the house for a short while before selling it to Richard "Boss" Croker.

Boss Croker is still a familiar name in the district. He had originated in Clonakilty, though his family had emigrated to the United States in the 1840's when he was a small boy. He had made a large amount of money in dubious circumstances in New York before leaving America in a hurry for England. Having failed to break into the social circles in England he acquired Glencairn in 1904 and moved to Ireland where his lavish spending made its mark. He set up racing stables at Glencairn and assembled a large area of land between Glencairn and Ballyogan Road that had been in various ownerships. Here he laid out The Gallops for training his race horses. The Gallops remained in use for its original purpose until comparatively recently, in the latter years as the McGrath gallops, before being developed for housing and shopping.

Architecturally, there was one major drawback to Croker's spending spree at Glencairn. He engaged the well known architect, James Franklin Fuller, to carry out extensive additions and alterations to Glencairn which, together with his stable block and other buildings, was completed by 1906. While J F Fuller had his own qualities as an architect, the loss of a Woodward-designed house was extremely unfortunate.

Greenfield House

We have seen earlier that in the seventeenth century David Morris had a farm of 46 acres on the land to the north east of the river at Kilgobbin, extending down where Ballyogan Road now runs. There must have been a farm house on this site at that time and also in the eighteenth century when the land passed through the various hands mentioned previously. John Rocque's map of County Dublin of 1760 shows a pair of parallel buildings in the position now occupied by Greenfield and its outbuildings and no other buildings are shown on the farm (see Figure 9). It seems logical to assume that the present site of Greenfield has been occupied by a house and outbuildings for at least three hundred years.

Greenfield ceased to be the farmhouse for the 46 acre farm when the Shea family stopped farming the property following the death of Margaret Shea in 1822 and the farm was split up into smaller plots. Her son and daughter, William and Alice, lived in the house until 1828 when William Shea moved to Dublin. Greenfield was left with about ten Irish plantation acres, equivalent to 16 statute acres or more than six hectares. During the rest of the nineteenth century the house had a number of occupiers including a member of the Richardson family, who lived there briefly in the 1860's. The present house was built at the end of the nineteenth century when Arthur Manly moved there from Clonlea in Murphystown.

Jamestown House

The original house to bear this name is now a picturesque ruin in the middle of Stepaside Golf Course. It was built by the Rourke or Rorke family in the late eighteenth century. Edward Rourke was a pin maker based in Dublin's Liberties. He was evidently a successful manufacturer with funds available to lend by way of mortgages. In 1780 he lent £400 to the Webbs of Kilgobbin and in 1787 this was still outstanding when he lent a further £200. A little later in the year he took Edward Webb to court in an attempt to recoup his money. In May 1791 Edward Webb leased almost thirty acres to Edward Rourke and it is possible that this transaction was part of the deal for settling the outstanding debts. The land adjoined part of Jamestown that was already occupied by Edward Rourke. In 1781 he had lent £200 to John Nowlan, a farmer who held a considerable tract of land at Jamestown. Seven years later, John Nowlan moved closer to the city and sold his farm at Jamestown to Edward Rourke for £612. This was only a leasehold interest, of course, with eighteen years left to run, and the lands were subject to an annual rent of £182.

It appears that Edward Rourke acquired the land in order to build a fine house for himself and his wife, Margaret. The result was Jamestown House, a splendid Georgian house of fine, but comparatively modest, proportions

Page 95

that may be seen in ruins in the middle of Stepaside Golf Course. Edward Rorke did not survive long to enjoy it and was succeeded by his eldest son, John Rorke, who also continued the family business. Margaret Rorke survived until 1831. Edward Rourke had branched out and become more of a merchant than a manufacturer and John Rorke is also described as a merchant. John Rorke renewed his lease on the lands at Jamestown from the Hutchinson family in 1797, amounting to some 160 Irish acres, equivalent to more than 250 statute acres or in excess of 100 hectares. A couple of years later, John Rorke married Mary Lawless, though it is not certain whether she was related to the Lawlesses who were shortly to appear at Kilgobbin.

Over time, John Rorke took leases on various plots of land in the area around Kilgobbin and Murphystown. For reasons that are not clear but which may be connected with his business, John Rorke went bankrupt in 1818. As far as his Jamestown and Kilgobbin lands are concerned he was bailed out by his brother, Andrew Rorke. The lands were advertised for sale by the parties assigned to administer his estate and were bought by Andrew Rorke for £2,200. For this he acquired almost 170 acres together with the mansion house and all other buildings and improvements which the Rorkes had carried out. Andrew Rorke had not bought the property for his own use, but allowed his brother to continue in occupation. This was not purely an altruistic gesture, but more of a lending hand in a crisis. The arrangement was that John Rorke owed £3,000 to Andrew Rorke, secured on the property. By the late 1820's John Rorke had repaid this sum.

John Rorke died in about the late 1830's and the property was inherited by John Henry O'Rourke, probably his son. The family ran the property as a farm for many years afterwards. The house survived until the middle of the twentieth century and now its shell remains as an adornment to the golf course.

Kilgobbin Castle

The builder of the house known as Kilgobbin Castle was in the unusual position of being his own landlord! We have already seen how the Bayly family came to have a substantial interest in the land around the Kilgobbin area. However, as has already been mentioned, all of this land was leased to tenants and none was in the family's own hands. In June 1831, Emanuel J

and they retained an interest in the property for many years after that while farming land at Murphystown.

Kilgobbin Villa

The Shea family hived off part of their farm to John Richardson who was a mason and a builder. Kilgobbin Villa was built in the late eighteenth century and can be seen on Taylor's map of *The Environs of Dublin* published in 1816 (see Figure 10). Over the years the Richardson family has lived at Kilgobbin Villa, though at times it has been let to tenants. John Richardson ran a shop in the house until about the 1840's. The family began to farm land locally in the mid nineteenth century and gradually acquired leases of an increasingly large amount of property. Other houses in the locality have been occupied by various members of the Richardson family over the years, but Kilgobbin Villa and Clay Farm have remained their principal homes.

Larkfield

Larkfield formerly stood in large grounds on Ballyogan Road opposite the Leopardstown Valley shopping centre. It was another house that was built as a result of the break up of the farm formerly known as David Morris's farm following the death of Margaret Shea in the early 1820's. Her son and daughter, William and Alice Shea leased 33 plantation acres to George Frederick Mowlds, consisting of land on both sides of the Ballyogan Road. George F Mowlds built himself a villa which, in the style of the time, consisted of a single storey over basement. To the front he laid out a handsome lawn and around it he planted trees for shelter.

George Frederick Mowlds and his wife, Margaret, lived at Larkfield until his death in the early 1860's. He had run into financial difficulties late in his life and was insolvent at the time of his death. The property was sold by the Landed Estates Court in 1866 and the new owner split it up, separating the land on the opposite side of the road from the house. Larkfield then came into the hands of George Gresson, who lived at Glencairn, and it remained as part of the estate of the various subsequent occupiers of Glencairn while being let to tenants.

Lilliput

see *Lisieux*

Lisieux

Emor and Philip North acquired North Lodge (see below) and the 15½ acres that went with it in the 1770's. In 1789 Emor North conveyed the south-western portion of the land, known as Cottage Park, to a Dublin barrister named John O'Connor with a condition that he spend £100 on the premises within six months. John O'Connor responded by building a house which he called Lilliput. He sold the property in 1807 to Humphrey Minchin for £1200. In 1830 Walter Bourne issued Court proceedings against Humphrey Minchin for debts exceeding £1400. As a result, Minchin's property at Murphystown was put up for auction by the High Sheriff and the successful bidder was none other than Walter Bourne himself, who bought the house, by now with 19 acres, for £200. This price presumably reflected the outstanding debts. The Bourne family subsequently built a fine new house which they named Park Cottage, though it was sometimes still known as Cottage Park. The most eminent occupier of the house was Sir Francis MacCabe, a doctor who had made a name as Medical Member of the Prisons Board for Ireland and later as Medical Commissioner of the Local Government Board for Ireland. He served as a member of several government bodies such as the Royal Commission for Inquiring into the Death-rate for Dublin and Drainage and Sewerage of that City and he was knighted in 1892. The house is now known as Lisieux.

Moreen

The house known as Moreen dated from 1783 when William McKay acquired a lease of a farm known as Little Moreen that had previously been occupied by one of the Rinkle family that has a long association with the area. He gradually acquired other plots of land and came to hold a large area to the north and west of Sandyford village. The McKay family occupied the house until the 1850's, following which it had a number of occupiers, including the land surveyor, Joseph Henry Kincaid. The site of the house is now occupied by the Central Bank premises.

Mount Eagle

Mount Eagle, on Kilgobbin Road near Sandyford Cross, would seem to owe its origins to the Reverend William Flood of Kilgobbin, who took a lease of the property in 1793. At that time there were cabins and outbuildings on the premises and Rev. Flood seems to have built the house before leasing the property on to Robert Hyde. At that time the house came with 18 acres of land, though this was later greatly reduced to less than 1½ acres.

Murphystown Lodge

see *Clonlea*

North Lodge

North Lodge was close to Murphystown Road, on a site that is now part of the grounds of "Lisieux". The house seems to have originated in 1769 when Benjamin Daniel acquired some 15 or 16 acres at Murphystown. On this land the house was built, probably by Benjamin Daniel, though before long it was in the hands of Emor and Philip North, from whom it got its name. They do not seem to have occupied the house, but let it to tenants. This was the house that was acquired in 1802 by John Bellett, whose family was prominent in the area for the first half of the nineteenth century, until they sold their interest in the house in 1853. The house was acquired by the Bourne family who had built the adjoining house now known as Lisieux, and for a time the two houses co-existed. North Lodge was demolished in the late 1860's.

Oldtown House

This house was formerly the White House of Kilgobbin, the inn that formed the focus of the town after the demise of the castle. As we have seen, the inn appears to have been built in the late seventeenth century and served travellers passing along the road to Enniskerry throughout the eighteenth century. We have also seen that the inn was in the heart of the old town of Kilgobbin and so it was appropriate that in the nineteenth century the inn, now occupied as a private house, should be renamed *Oldtown House*. In

1823 it was acquired by Margaret Cuthbert, widow of Richard Cuthbert of Glasnevin. The land that came with the house lay on both sides of the road, with the lion's share being on the opposite side, close to the castle. She set about building houses on the property to provide her with an income from rents and she leased a substantial plot of land for the building of the house now known as Kilgobbin Castle. Oldtown House had a number of occupiers since becoming a private house and was substantially refurbished in the 1950's.

Park Cottage

see *Lisieux*

Sandyford House

The house of this name dates from the eighteenth century and would originally have been a farm house. Its most famous reputed occupant was Major Henry Sirr, Town Major of Dublin at the end of the eighteenth and beginning of the nineteenth century. It was Major Sirr who arrested both Lord Edward Fitzgerald (in 1798) and Robert Emmet (in 1803). It is local tradition in Sandyford that Major Sirr lived in this house and that it was under military guard to protect the Major from reprisals following his famous arrests. His official residence was in Dublin Castle, though there is no reason why he should not have a country retreat like many gentlemen of his day. If he did live here he seems to have rented the house rather than taking a lease as no deed is registered in his name in the Registry of Deeds in relation to this property.

Thornberry

This was one of the houses built by Margaret Cuthbert in the 1820's, though it appears that there were buildings on or near the site beforehand, as part of the town of Kilgobbin. The Cuthbert family let Thornberry to tenants for over fifty years and following the death of Cecilia Cuthbert the house was auctioned, the purchaser being a merchant named John Pitt.

Violet Hill

There was a dispensary in the Kilgobbin area from about the 1830's when legislation was passed to allow the funding of dispensaries out of public moneys. For most of the rest of the nineteenth century the local dispensary was in Stepaside while the dispensary doctors lived in a rented house. The dispensaries were the responsibility of the Poor Law Unions and, in 1879, legislation was passed to give them new powers to provide dispensaries. The Guardians of the Poor of Rathdown Union took advantage of this act in 1892 when a little over two statute acres was acquired on Kilgobbin Road. A loan of £1,200 was obtained from the Board of Works for the project and by 1894 a new dispensary had been built, along with a medical officer's residence. The first occupant was Dr William S Mackay. He had been medical officer of the local dispensary for about fifteen years at that stage and continued at Violet Hill until about 1927, making almost fifty years of service to the local community!

Washington Lodge

In 1771, William Webb leased almost twelve acres to David Fitzgerald, a Dublin surgeon. David Fitzgerald built a house which he named Washington Lodge. It has been suggested in the past that this house was named after the writer Washington Irving, however this is not the case as it was built before the writer was born and was known as Washington Lodge at least as early as June 1790. The reality must be that Washington Lodge was named after George Washington and in honouring the hero of the American revolution David Fitzgerald was in advance of even the American people, who did not start to build Washington DC until 1791. Precisely when he gave it the name may never be known, but it would not have been from the very beginning. David Fitzgerald leased the property in March 1771 and the house would have been built immediately. It was certainly there by 1777 when Taylor and Skinner surveyed the road to Powerscourt and included the house on their map of the road published in the following year in their volume *Maps of the Roads of Ireland* (Figure 13).

Washington Lodge was to the south of Kilgobbin and to the east of Stepaside. The access to the house was via the driveway which leads to Kilgobbin Cottage and Clay Farm and David Fitzgerald had a right of way

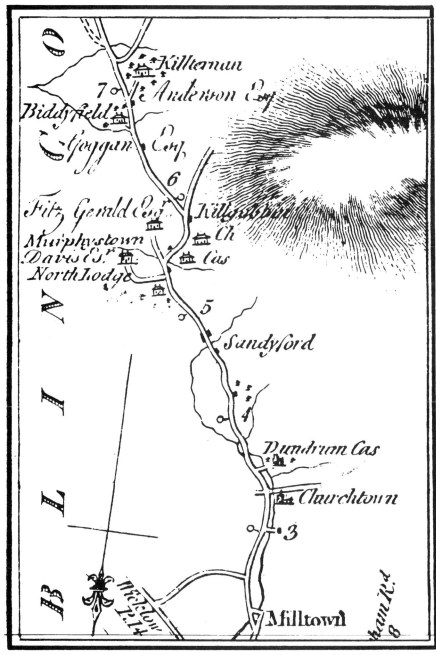

Figure 12. from Taylor and Skinner's Map of the Roads of Ireland (1777) [enlarged]

over this lane. Following David Fitzgerald's death it was inherited by his four daughters who let the property to tenants. The tenants wanted the property for farming as it came with some 62 statute acres. In fact, even by the end of the eighteenth century David Fitzgerald appears to have been living at Milltown. Washington Lodge was not cared for and became dilapidated by the 1860's and twenty years later it was in ruins. It survives today as a mass of granite rubble hidden beneath a thicket of blackthorn and bramble at the side of a field.

Woodside

There has been a house at Woodside for a considerable time. The lands of Sandyford, The Wood and Barnakilly were leased by Thomas Jones to James Atkinson in 1699 and correspond to Sandyford, Woodside and Barnacullia. The remnants of the wood itself remain as Fitzsimons Wood near Blackglen Road. The holding was comparatively large and must have had its own farmhouse and outbuildings from the time of the lease in 1699, though the earliest positive mention was in 1736 when the land was leased along with "all buildings and improvements erected thereon". This does not necessarily imply recent building, nor does it imply that there had been no buildings there before.

The earliest map of the area is John Rocque's map of 1760 which shows Woodside very clearly (Figure 9). It appears as a very substantial block of buildings in precisely the position that it occupies today, thereby showing that the present site has been in continuous use since the at least the early eighteenth century, and probably since the seventeenth.

The family that occupied Woodside for the longest period was the Hastings family. John Hastings acquired the property in 1836 and it remained in the family for the next seventy years before his son sold it. It was his son, William C Hastings, that added the front part to the house to give it the appearance that it has today.

Countess Markievicz of Blackglen

While the house associated locally with Countess Markievicz does not rank among the finer mansions of the district, the stature of the Countess in history makes it worthwhile recounting her associations with the area. It is well known locally that she had a cottage just off Blackglen Road. This was up a laneway just down the hill from the sliding rock. It was a two-roomed cottage, semi-detached, the other portion being a bit larger.

Count and Countess Markievicz lived at Rathgar. Both were accomplished painters, the Countess having studied at Slade and in Paris, where she had met the Count. According to one of the Countess's biographers, Anne Marreco, it was because of her painting that she rented the cottage at Black Glen in 1906, from her friends, the Fitzsimons. This biographer maintains that it was here that Constance Markievicz became converted to the Nationalist cause, giving the cottage a greater importance in her life than is recognised elsewhere. Apparently, the cottage had previously been rented by Pádraic Colum. If this is the case it may have been for a period after 1903 when he was granted a scholarship for study, and when he may have retreated from the bustle of daily life to pursue his studies, freed from his job with the railway. When he vacated the cottage he is supposed to have left various issues of magazines such as *Sinn Féin* and *The Peasant*. Constance Markievicz is said to have read these and was appalled at the injustices suffered by those not lucky enough to share her background amongst the landed gentry.

A later biographer, Diana Norman, disputes this version of the story, pointing out that it makes out that the Countess was naive and impulsive. It is likely, though, that while Countess Markievicz's conversion was more subtle and gradual, the influence of magazines may well had some effect on her outlook and helped in some way to harden her resolve to change the system. While the Countess's connection with the area is indisputable, there is less evidence for Pádraic Colum's presence at the cottage and if he had a tenancy at all it would seem to have been a very short one.

Once she had become a convert to the cause of socialism and nationalism, Countess Markievicz retained the use of the cottage and used it to further her work. The district was still comparatively remote and made an excellent training ground for her young recruits in Fianna Éireann, an organisation for boys which she founded in 1909. These boys were taught drilling and the use of arms on the hill slopes around the cottage. While the Countess was not involved in the Howth gun running, some of the rifles were brought to the cottage the next day and she and her helpers assisted in smuggling them into Dublin. During the 1916 Rising the Countess was in the thick of the fighting, but her cottage was occupied by James Connolly's wife, who waited for news while she was able to see the smoke from the city from the hillside nearby.

Constance Markievicz kept the cottage until around 1919, when her financial position, coupled with her intensive work on behalf of her constituents in the Liberties and the fact that she was frequently on the run from the authorities, would have made it difficult to keep a holiday home. In fact, she did not even have a home of her own at this period and lived as a guest in the house of colleagues in the cause.

In more recent years both the Countess's cottage and the adjoining one became ruinous. The Countess's portion was lived in until the early 1940's and was demolished in the 1970's as being unsafe. The other part followed suit in the early 1980's.

Labourers cottages and the Rathdown Rural District Council

Balally Terrace: two Storey Rathdown Cottages

Until the mid 19th century there was no alternative to private housing. Anyone who did not own property had to rent it from a landlord. The alternative was squatting, which involved putting up a crude cabin illegally on common land. As we have seen, there was frequently a chain of landlords and this often meant that a labourer would rent land and put up a cabin for himself along with other cabins which he would sub let in order to help with paying the rent. The quality of these homes could be very poor and security of tenure was often shaky. From the middle of the century, philanthropic bodies started to appear that would provide good quality housing at reasonable rents. However, these tended to cater for artisans rather than labourers and were mainly confined to the urban areas.

The first moves towards public sector housing started a little later. The Labourers (Ireland) Act of 1883 allowed local authorities to build cottages for labourers and to charge the cost to the rates. At that time the local authority in our area was the Rathdown Union, based at the workhouse at Loughlinstown and dealing with the area from Rathfarnham to Delgany. The Rathdown Union did not venture into this field and it was not until the early years of this century that public housing was provided in this locality. From 1898 there was a two-tier system of local government with Dublin County Council as the upper tier and, in our area, Rathdown No. 1 Rural District Council as the other tier. Rathdown No. 1 RDC had responsibility for the part of the old Rathdown Union that lay within County Dublin. Rathdown No. 2 RDC dealt with north east Wicklow.

From 1902, Rathdown No. 1 RDC started to acquire sites for house building. The first houses in our district, at Kilgobbin and Murphystown, were occupied by 1903. A second wave followed in 1905/6 including more in Kilgobbin and Murphystown and others on Ballyogan Road. Two pairs of houses were built in Sandyford village at this time. A new law, the Labourers (Ireland) Act, 1906, allowed extra money to be provided for labourers cottages. Rathdown No. 1 RDC was already in full spate providing cottages, but a third phase of house building followed and these were occupied by 1909, including four more on Ballyogan Road, another two in Sandyford village and others in Kilgobbin and Murphystown. The five at Blackglen Road near Countess Markievicz's cottage followed soon afterwards.

By 1910 the Council had provided more than forty houses for labourers in our area. Most of them were single storey cottages, but quite a few were two storey. The two storey Rathdown cottage is very distinctive, having half-dormers on the upper floor, with a gently forward-sloping slate roof over the dormer. These were usually built in pairs, though sometimes singly. Balally Terrace is unusual not only in that it is a terrace, but in not facing directly on to the road. All of these houses were well built with the good quality architectural detail that was in vogue at the turn of the century, and they would gave been a great contrast to the accommodation the tenants had occupied before. The weekly rent was generally about 1 shilling and 9 pence.

Single Storey Rathdown Cottage, Murphystown Road

As would be expected, most of the occupiers of these houses were labourers. The majority were agricultural labourers, though some were general labourers. A few followed other occupations such as a coachman living in one cottage at Kilgobbin, a boot maker at Murphystown and two gardeners occupying cottages on Ballyogan Road. Invariably the tenants were married couples, usually, but not always, with children. The average number of children in 1911 was four, though quite a number of families had six or more.

Many of these Rathdown cottages are now privately owned, having been bought out by their tenants. They continue to form an important part of the history of the district, marking the first move into decent quality houses for many of the labourers of our area.

12. PLACE NAMES

Among the names which we have found in the locality are the townlands - Kilgobbin, Jamestown, Woodside, Barnacullia, Newtown Little, Ballyedmonduff, Balally and Murphystown. Other local names include Black Glen, Hillcrest, Stepaside, Sandyford and Ballawley.

Of these, Kilgobbin is the most straight forward, as we have seen - the church of Gobán. Jamestown is more obscure, but comparatively simple, and we have seen how the saint's name was confused over the sharing of the same holy day. Ballyedmonduff - Black Edmund's townland, is also fairly easy, though it begs the questions as to who was Black Edmund.

Who was the Murphy of Murphystown? The name was originally Mulchanstown, or Ballymolchan, though at least as early as the beginning of the eighteenth century the name was being given, unofficially, as Murphystown. It was the mid eighteenth century before the name began to be used officially in documents, though usually with the alternatives of Mulchanstown or Ballymolchan. When the Ordnance Survey set down the boundaries of the townlands in the 1830's Murphystown townland was carved into three, and these survive today as the townlands of Murphystown, Mulchanstown and Blackthorn. Blackthorn lies between the other two and is now mainly occupied by Sandyford Industrial Estate and Stillorgan Industrial Park. The name is curious, as the farm known as Blackthorn was originally part of Balally, near Sandyford village, and not Murphystown. Mulchanstown is now a fairly geometric and unnatural shape, its boundaries coinciding with the Stillorgan Reservoirs. Originally the boundary was somewhat wider and less geometric. The position of Blackthorn between Mulchanstown and Murphystown conceals the original connection of these two townlands. There are various references to Mulchanstown Castle in the histories and these would refer to Murphystown Castle for the reasons given above.

Woodside, Barnacullia and Sandyford come together as a trio. From at least as early as the end of the seventeenth century three plots of land were included together in leases - Sandyford, The Wood and Barnakilly. Later these take on their more modern names of Sandyford, Woodside and Barnacullia. While Woodside and Barnacullia seem to both refer to the ancient woodland now known as Fitzsimon's Wood, Sandyford does not, and any attempt to give it the name *Taobh na Coille,* as is somethimes done, is a denial of Sandyford's separate existence from Woodside.

Balally and Ballawley come from the same origin, reputed to be the "Townland of Olaf". As with Murphystown, several alternative spellings seem to have been used in the early eighteenth century though, curiously, "Balally" was not one of them. The present day spelling stems from the rather high-handed views of the Ordnance Survey in the 1830's. While their surveyor observed that Ballawley was more correct, Ballally was offered as an alternative. However, the eminent John O'Donovan, in his capacity as antiquarian to the Ordnance Survey, decided that the latter was too much like Ball Alley and opted for Balally despite the lack of precedent for the spelling.

Hillcrest and Newtown Little are comparatively modern names, while Stepaside is an eighteenth century name as we have already seen. Various possible origins of the name Stepaside have been put forward. The Reverend O Murchoe in the 1920's supposed that it was named after an inn sign, while the Ordnance Survey reported in the 1830's that the local inhabitants explained that it was a corruption of "Steepside". This is possible, given the topography and that the origin of the name was almost within living memory at that time.

St Patrick's Well is in the grounds of a house on the right hand side of the road leading from Stepaside to Kilternan. Two houses here have been given the name St Patrick's Well, and a third is called Well Park. The name was originally applied to all of the land in the townland of Jamestown lying on that side of the road, amounting to some 75 hectares, or almost 190 statute acres. There are wells dedicated to St Patrick all over Ireland, including two in Dublin city centre. The origins of this one are obscure, particularly as the name is at variance with the dedication of the local Early Christian church.

Finally, Black Glen is a name which appears in the eighteenth century, and probably predates that period. The name refers to a part of Balally on the edge of the townland next to Barnacullia and was spelt, in the manner of the day, "Black Glynn".

13. CONCLUSION

We have seen how the area we have been examining was occupied in pre-historic times and a significant amount of Neolithic remains have been found in the district. More evidently, particularly in the immediate vicinity of Kilgobbin, there seems to have been a strong presence of people in the district during the Bronze Age. The earliest tangible remains date from the Early Christian period, in the form of the church sites and, from the Viking period, the cross and fragments of grave slabs at Kilgobbin.

Within historic times, there is information about some of the occupiers of land in the early period after the arrival of the Normans, but no buildings survive that date from that time. The fragment of the gatehouse that survives from Carrickmines Castle and the banks and ditches alongside it would represent the earliest buildings from that era. Kilgobbin Castle is a survivor from the later medieval era, and carries with it the reminder that Kilgobbin saw its share of action in the troubled times of the rebellion that started in 1641. Murphystown Castle is of a similar age. Also from the late medieval period we have in the locality the most substantial remains of the old Pale ditch that survive in County Dublin, and one of the finest stretches of the ditch anywhere.

We have heard how the area started to take up its present shape later in the seventeenth century and many of the landholdings and farms owe their origins to that time, particularly in the area around Kilgobbin. Possibly also dating to the seventeenth century, if not earlier, is the town of Kilgobbin which had been demoted to a residential village or hamlet by the early nineteenth century.

A variety of gentry and nobility have had an interest in the district over the years, but most of them lived elsewhere, merely holding land here for investment purposes. In the late eighteenth century the first of the houses of the gentry started to appear when North Lodge was built at Murphystown and David Fitzgerald, a Dublin surgeon, built himself a house at Kilgobbin followed, a few years later, by Edward Rourke, a Dublin merchant and manufacturer, who built Jamestown House in the 1790's.

The older houses which survive in Kilgobbin village, and give it its essential character, started to be built in the late eighteenth century when Kilgobbin House and Kilgobbin Villa were built. In the nineteenth century these were augmented by villas such as Larkfield, Elmfield, Kilgobbin Castle and Kilgobbin Cottage, while some of the earlier farms such as Greenfield and Woodside were enlarged or rebuilt. Other houses dating from this time include Lilliput, Clonlea and Moreen.

This trend of building villas gradually changed the nature of the inhabitants. In the eighteenth century the local people had been predominantly involved in agriculture, but as the nineteenth century progressed there came an increasing number of others. These included a growing number of stone cutters as well as other people who worked locally such as teachers, dispensary doctors, postmasters, grocers, publicans and a few servants. They also included progressively more people who worked in the city in professional or managerial jobs. There were judges living at Glencairn and Fernhill, and elsewhere solicitors and barristers lived. There were also stockbrokers, accountants, commercial travellers, land agents and suchlike.

The introduction of new houses has continued to today, with newer houses at Kilgobbin Heights, Kilcross, Sandyford Hall and St Patrick's Park adding to the variety already existing in the area, while the older houses are mainly occupied by people working in the city as they were a hundred years ago. Along with this, the essential farming activities still continue as they did three hundred years ago when Thomas Jones was granting leases on the property.

14. BIBLIOGRAPHY

The following sources have been consulted in the writing of this history:

Anon. **St Mary's 1829-1979: 150th Jubilee Year: Souvenir Brochure** St Mary's Parish, (1979)

Archaeological Survey of Ireland, Office of Public Works **Sites and Monuments Record for the County of Dublin** Office of Public Works (1988)

Ball, Francis Elrington and Hamilton, Everard **The Parish of Taney** (1895)

Ball, Francis Elrington *Mount Merrion and its History* **Journal of the Royal Society of Antiquaries of Ireland** Vol. 28 (1898)

Ball, Francis Elrington *Some Notes on the Townland of Murphystown, in the County of Dublin* **The Irish Builder** Vol. XL, No. 917, 1 March 1898, p. 33-4

Ball, Francis Elrington *Some Notes on the Townland of Balally, in the County of Dublin* **The Irish Builder** Vol. XL, No. 918, 15 March 1898, p. 41-2

Ball, Francis Elrington **The History of the County Dublin Vol. I** (1902), **Vol. II** (1903), **Vol. III** (1905)

Barry, T B **The Archaeology of Medieval Ireland** Routledge (1987)

Borlase, Edmund **History of the Irish Rebellion of 1641-9** (1680)

Boylan, Henry **A Dictionary of Irish Biography** Gill and Macmillan (1988)

Cantwell, Brian **Memorial Transcriptions: Glencullen old Churchyard** (unpublished) (1981)

Census of Ireland, 1659

Census of Ireland, 1821-1911

Civil Survey, (1654)

Cronin, Patrick **Boss Croker of New York City and Glencairn** Foxrock Local History Club Publication No. 8 (1983)

D'Alton, John **The History of the County of Dublin** Hodges and Smith, (1838)

Debrett **Baronetage, Knightage and Companionage** (1900)

Devitt, Rev M *The Rampart of the Pale* **Journal of the County Kildare Archaeological Society** Vol. III (1899-1902)

Dix, E R McC *The Lesser Castles in the County Dublin: Kilgobbin* **The Irish Builder** Vol. XXXIX , pp. 86, 95, 199 (1897)

Dix, E R McC *The Lesser Castles in the County Dublin: Murphystown* **The Irish Builder** Vol. XXXIX, p. 199 (1897)

Doherty, J E and Hickey, D J **A Dictionary of Irish History 1800-1980** Gill and Macmillan (1987)

Doherty, J E and Hickey, D J **A Chronology of Irish History since 1500** Gill and Macmillan (1989)

Donnelly, Most Rev M. **A Short history of Some Dublin Parishes, Part IV: Parishes of Monkstown, Kingstown, Glasthule and Dalkey (1906)**

Donnelly, Most Rev M. **A Short history of Some Dublin Parishes, Part V: The Parishes of Sandyford and Glencullen, Killiney, Little Bray, Cabinteely (1906)**

Dublin Journal No. 2487 (8-12 January 1750/51)

Dublin Public Libraries **Directory of Graveyards in the Dublin area: an Index and Guide to Burial Records** (1988)

Egan, Dr Michael J S **Dublin City and County Graveyards** The Ireland Branch of the Irish Genealogical Research Society (1989) (unpublished)

Ellis, Eilish *Murphystown* **Three Rock Panorama** Vol. 16, No. 11, (Dec. 1990)

Ellis, Eilish *Kilgobbin Castle* **Three Rock Panorama** Vol. 18, No. 2, (Feb. 1992)

Ellis, Eilish *Stepaside* **Three Rock Panorama** Vol. 18, No. 6, (June 1992)

Ellis, Steven G **Reform and Revival: English Government in Ireland,**

1470-1534 (London, 1984)

Ellis, Steven G **Tudor Ireland: Crown, Community and the Conflict of Cultures, 1470-1603**

Goodbody, Rob *Murphystown Castle* **Rathmichael Historical Record** (pending)

Goodbody, Rob *Pale Ditch in South County Dublin* **Archaeology Ireland** Vol. 7, No. 3 (Autumn 1993).

Healy, Patrick **Kilgobbin, Kilternan and the Enniskerry Road** (unpublished lecture) (n.d.)

Healy, Patrick **A report on the importance of an Earthwork believed to be part of the Pale ditch at Balally, Co Dublin** (unpublished) (September 1978)

Healy, P **Report on Circular Mound and Castle at Kilgobbin, Co. Dublin** (unpublished) (July 1983)

Healy, P **Report on Carrickmines Castle, Co Dublin** (unpublished) (July 1983)

Hickey, D J, and Doherty, J E **A Dictionary of Irish History 1800 - 1980** Gill and Macmillan (1987)

Historic Manuscripts Commission **Papers in the Collection of the Earl of Rosse, Birr Castle** Report no. 2, Appendix

Historic Manuscripts Commission **The Manuscripts of the Marquis of Ormonde Preserved at The Castle, Kilkenny, Vol. 1** (1895) Fourteenth Report, Appendix, Part VII

Keeley, Valerie *Taylorsgrange: Portal Tomb* in Cotter, Claire (ed.) **Excavations 1985** Irish Academic Publications (1986)

Keeley, Valerie *Brehon's Chair, Taylorsgrange* in Bennett, Isabel (ed.) **Excavations 1987** Organisation of Irish Archaeologists (1988)

Kennedy, Dermot **The Battle of Deansgrange, 1642** Foxrock Local History Club Publication No. 19 (1986)

Kilternan Parish **Kilternan Church 1826-1976**

Landed Estates Court information in National Archive, Bishop Street

Lewis, Samuel **A Topographical Dictionary of Ireland (1837)**

Local History Group, Sandyford ICA Guild **Beneath the Granite Throne** Irish Countrywomans Association (1992)

Lydon, James **Ireland in the later Middle Ages** Gill and Macmillan (1973)

Marreco, Anne **The Rebel Countess** Corgi Books (1969)

McNeill, T E *The origins of Tower Houses* **Archaeology Ireland** Vol. 6, No. 1, (Spring 1992)

Mills, James *The Norman Settlement in Leinster - The Cantreds near Dublin* **Journal of the Royal Society of Antiquaries of Ireland** Vol. 26 (1894)

Mount, Charles and Keeley, Valerie *An Early Medieval Strap Tag from Balally, Co Dublin* **Journal of the Royal Society of Antiquaries of Ireland** Vol. 120 (1990)

Murphy, Rev Denis *The Pale* **Journal of the County Kildare Archaeological Society** Vol. II, (1896-99)

National Museum of Ireland, Irish Antiquities Division: files on archaeological finds

Newman Johnson, D **Dublin Castles** The Resource Source No. 13 (1988)

Norman, Diana **Terrible Beauty: A Life of Constance Markievicz 1868-1927** Hodder & Stoughton (1987)

O Dwyer, Frederick, and Williams, J *Benjamin Woodward* in Kennedy, Tom, **Victorian Dublin** Albertine Kennedy Publishing with the Dublin Arts Festival (1980)

O hEailidhe, P *Decorated Stones at Kilgobbin, Co Dublin* **Journal of the Royal Society of Antiquaries of Ireland** Vol. 114, (1984)

O Keefe, Tadhg *Medieval Frontiers and Fortification: The Pale and its Evolution* in Aalen, F H A and Whelan, Kevin **DUBLIN City and County: From Prehistory to Present** Geography Publications, (1992)

O Murchoe, Rev. Thomas **A History of Kilternan and Kilgobbin** edited by Rev. J B Leslie. Church of Ireland Printing and Publishing Company (1934)

O Reilly, Patrick J *The Christian Sepulchral Leacs and Free-Standing Crosses of the Dublin Half-Barony of Rathdown* **Journal of the Royal Society of Antiquaries of Ireland** Vol. XXXI (1901)

Ordnance Survey of Ireland **Field Name Book, Parish of Kilgobbin** (1830's)

Ordnance Survey of Ireland **Field Name Book, Parish of Taney** (1836)

Ordnance **Survey of Ireland 6" to the mile Dublin** sheets 22, 23, 25 and 26 (1843)

Pilkington, R K C *Kilgobbin Church* **Rathmichael Historical Record** (1984)

Registry of Deeds: Various deeds from 1708.

Rocque, John **An Actual Survey of the county of Dublin** (1760)

Rowe, V *To Dundrum and Enniskerry by Horse Power* Three Rock Panorama

Ryan, Nicholas M **Sparkling Granite: The Story of the Granite Working People of the Three Rock Region of County Dublin** Stone Publishing (1992)

Taylor, George and Skinner, Andrew **Maps of the Roads of Ireland** (1778)

Taylor, John **Map of the Environs of Dublin** (1816)

Tempest, H G *The Pale Ditch in County Louth* **Journal of the Co Louth Archaeological Society** Vol. X, No. 2 (1941)

Thom's Directories 1845 onwards

Turner, Kathleen **If You Seek Monuments** Rathmichael Historical Society (1984)

Turner, Kathleen **Rathmichael: A Parish History** Select Vestry, Rathmichael Parish (1987)

Valuations: Various valuations in connection with Tithes and the Poor Law

INDEX

D'Alton, John	21, 46
Daniel, Benjamin	101
Darley, Alderman Frederick	46, 59, 80, 92
Darley, Edmund S	80
Darley family	92-93
Darley, Judge	80
Davis, Jeffrey	65
Davis, Captain William	65
Dawson, John	58, 60, 61, 71, 72
Deane, Thomas	93
Deansgrange, battle	34
Deansgrange burial ground	4
Deansgrange cemetery	47
Dispensary	78, 103
Dix, E R McC	21, 23
Dolmens	5, 6
Donnybrook church	43
Down Survey	17, 23
Doyle family	65-66
Dublin County Council	12
Dublin Paving Board	89
Dundrum	9, 15
Dundrum castle	16, 20, 34
Early Christian period	6, 7, 113
Elizabeth I	33
Elmfield House	61, 64, 65, 92, 114
Enniskerry	74
Enniskerry Road	75, 79, 80, 87
Eustace, Sir Maurice	55, 56, 57, 66
Eyre family	58
Fenian rising	82
Fern Hill	59, 80, 92-93
Field, Rose	75
Fitzgerald, David	59, 60, 66-67, 103, 113
Fitzgerald, Miss	66
Fitzsimon family	51, 106